THE POLITICAL ECONOMY
OF THE WELFARE STATE

CRITICAL TEXTS IN SOCIAL WORK AND THE WELFARE STATE

General Editor: Peter Leonard

Published

Paul Corrigan and Peter Leonard: SOCIAL WORK PRACTICE
UNDER CAPITALISM: A MARXIST APPROACH
Norman Ginsburg: CLASS, CAPITAL AND SOCIAL POLICY
Ian Gough: THE POLITICAL ECONOMY OF THE WELFARE STATE

Forthcoming

Steve Bolger, Paul Corrigan, Nick Frost and Jan McNamara:
WORKING IN THE STATE: THE FAMILY AND SOCIAL WORK
Christopher Jones: SOCIAL WORK PROFESSIONALISATION:
A CRITIQUE
Geoffrey Pearson: IDEOLOGICAL CRISIS IN SOCIAL WORK

THE POLITICAL ECONOMY OF THE WELFARE STATE

IAN GOUGH

M

First edition 1979
Reprinted 1979, 1980

Published by
THE MACMILLAN PRESS LTD
London and Basingstoke
Associated companies in Delhi Dublin
Hong Kong Johannesburg Lagos Melbourne
New York Singapore and Tokyo

Printed in Great Britain
by Unwin Brothers Limited
The Gresham Press, Old Woking, Surrey

British Library Cataloguing in Publication Data

Gough, Ian
    The political economy of the welfare state.
    —(Critical texts in social work and the
    welfare state).
    1. Great Britain—Economic policy—1945–
    I. Title   II. Series
    330.9′41′0857   HC256.6

ISBN 0–333–21599–0

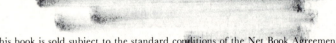

CONTENTS

EDITOR'S INTRODUCTION

As a form of ideological mystification, the concept of the welfare state has played a most significant role in post-war Britain. The major political parties have conducted their debate largely around questions about the purposes, costs and effectiveness of the various state services and activities which are generally seen as comprising the welfare or social service operations of the state. But although there has certainly been *debate*, it has been conducted within very narrow confines and has reflected, on the whole, a most naive, ahistorical and unscientific appreciation of the political and economic imperatives which determine the activities of an advanced capitalist state. Of course, the poverty and irrelevance of much of this debate— for example, between Fabians and monetarists—have not been the result simply of a failure to comprehend the complexities and contradictions of the economy, but have been, ultimately, the outcome of a commitment (sometimes faltering) to the dominant ideology which supports the economy.

Debate and discussion about the welfare state has been conducted *within* bourgeois political categories and bourgeois academic disciplines—categories and disciplines which effectively limit the debate and contribute to a continuing intellectual legitimation of existing social arrangements. The concept of the welfare state as a humane response to need has performed an invaluable ideological function in the control and discipline of working-class populations, for in the name of 'welfare' much can be achieved which would be impossible by more direct methods of repression. At a material level the ideological mystification of 'welfare' is embedded in the concrete operations of the services themselves, in the assessment of 'need', in the evaluation of 'effectiveness', in the state organisation of 'participation', and in many other aspects.

The ideological nature of both the discussion and the practical operation of the welfare state has quite clearly been reflected in academic study and professional training. Thus, within economics, social administration, social work education and, to a somewhat lesser extent, sociology, analysis of the welfare state has been dominated by taken-for-granted assumptions about both the economy and the state. Whilst the work of some mainstream writers, such as Richard Titmuss, has certainly contributed to a re-evaluation of the welfare state, nevertheless their lack of the basic conceptual tools with which to construct an adequate *social* theory of the welfare state has left their analyses without a proper scientific foundation. In more recent years the exclusive domination of varieties of mainstream Fabian and conservative approaches to the welfare state has given way to a more confused and conflict-ridden situation. This has been not only because of the inevitable disillusionment which is accompanying public expenditure cuts as a reflection of a deep-seated economic crisis, but also because alternatives to the previously dominant approaches to the welfare state are steadily emerging.

Without question the most significant of these alternative approaches are those which are firmly based in an historical and comparative method and which are contributing to the articulation of a political economy of the advanced capitalist state and the social services apparatus that it develops. This creation and elaboration of a specifically Marxist perspective on the welfare state is emerging in many places—for example, in the Conference of Socialist Economists. Ian Gough published a seminal paper on public expenditure in the welfare field in the *New Left Review* in 1975 which created immense interest and debate and contributed substantially to furthering the Marxist perspective. He has now been able to develop and revise his ideas more fully and to produce a book which most appropriately appears early in a series specifically devoted to extending Marxist theory: 'Critical Texts in Social Work and the Welfare State'. This book will prove to be an important break-through in the analysis of the welfare state and the origins and implications of its present crisis. Here the ground is laid for a political economy of the welfare state which is not confined by the traditional disciplinary boundaries of economics, political science, social administration or sociology, but which attempts to grasp its development *holistically* as a feature of the state in advanced capitalism.

What Gough's book clearly demonstrates is that a scientific approach to the welfare state must include considerable emphasis on economic analysis and the careful use of historical materials. Thus, an understanding of the laws of motion of capital is the means by which we can chart the development of productive forces, the concentration of capital and the establishment of a world monopolist economic system which determines the parameters of social policy within Western countries. Again, documentation of the historical origins and growth of the working class is essential to an understanding of the part played by class struggle in the development of social policy and to a tactical and strategic appreciation of the extent to which the apparatus of the welfare state itself can today be considered as an arena of class struggle. But mention of the laws of motion of capital on the one hand and class struggle on the other brings us to a central problem in Marxist analysis: the understanding of contradiction. Contradictions exist in the material world and are reflected in the world of ideas; the welfare state can be envisaged *both* as functional to the needs of capitalist development *and* as the result of the political struggles of the organised working class. This material contradiction is reflected in the attempts of Marxists to understand it, to grasp the dynamic relationship between historical laws and tendencies and the collective intentions of men and women confronting these laws. All sensitive and careful Marxist writing on the state and on the economy has to walk a tightrope between crude functionalism and starry-eyed voluntarism—at its extreme, between seeing the welfare state as wholly oppressive and seeing it as a bastion of socialism within a capitalist economy. In this book one senses a real dialectical grasp of the relation between function and struggle, one which will give rise to considerable debate, especially among Marxist economists and students of social policy.

Many will find this a contentious book; both Marxists and non-Marxists will want to argue with it as well as experiencing a substantial gain in understanding as a result of reading it. It will place, more firmly than ever, the contribution of Marxist analysis on the agenda of study and debate about the welfare state. But Marxists write not only to understand the world, but to change it, and so the scientific advance represented by this book must not only form a basis for the critique of dominant ideologies of the welfare state, but, very importantly, contribute to the practice of workers within the welfare state apparatus who are attempting to further the class struggle within it.

PETER LEONARD

PREFACE

The phrase 'the welfare state' entered our vocabulary during and immediately after the Second World War. The rash of social legislation enacted in Britain in the 1940s appeared to mark the dawn of a new era variously interpreted as 'post-industrial society', the 'mixed economy', 'welfare society' or even 'democratic welfare capitalism'. Certainly the post-war period has witnessed a profound transformation in economy and society, and in the role of the modern state. But now the tide appears to be turning, and it may well be that with hindsight the period from the 1940s to the early 1970s will be seen as the golden age of the welfare state, as a rather abnormal period associated with the 'long boom' of the advanced capitalist world.

Certainly the signs of crisis are everywhere to be seen. In 1974 the capitalist world entered its most profound economic recession since the 1930s and at the time of writing the prospects for another long boom are distinctly unpromising. In the welfare field, social expenditure is being cut back whilst here and abroad a rising tide of criticism engulfs the major institutions of the welfare state. The goals of liberal education are questioned, social workers are villified in the right-wing press, and a welfare backlash develops against the poor, 'scroungers', unemployed youth and coloured people whilst a 'taxation backlash' develops against the ever-growing level of state impositions. On right and left the earlier belief in the harmonious progress of welfare capitalism recedes.

Sociology, according to Alvin Gouldner, is the child of the welfare state. If so, the sickness of the parent has infected its progeny; and not only sociology but all the social sciences reflect the present crisis in the welfare state. In economics, for example, Keynesianism retreats in disarray whilst a strident anti-collectivist, free-market ideology has a field day, reiterating the impossibility of modifying economic laws or 'human nature' by means of welfare policies. Less

confidently, social administration and the Fabian tradition is reduced
to counterposing a system of priorities based on need to those of
the market, subject to one small condition: a strong economy is
a necessary prerequisite for a humane society and, to strengthen
the economy, anti-humanitarian and anti-welfare measures may
indeed be necessary. At the same time, others bemoan the threat
which the welfare state poses to parliamentary democracy.

We approach the 1980s, then, with an endemic crisis not only
in the capitalist economic system and the welfare state, but also
in the ability of social science to understand these changes. This
book attempts to disengage itself from the fetters of conventional
social-science disciplines by adopting a totally different perspective
on the welfare state: that of Marxist political economy. It is no
coincidence that a revival of political economy is taking place at
the present time, as the real world of capitalism enters a new phase
which orthodox disciplines are ill equipped to explain. Whether the
alternative advanced here represents a step forward in our understanding of the welfare state is for the reader—and the future—to
judge.

Many friends have contributed in various ways to this book. In
particular, for detailed and constructive comments on virtually an
entire first draft, I would like to thank Risto Erasaari, Norman
Ginsburg, John Harrison, John Holloway, Phil Leeson, Vicente
Navarro, David Purdy, Len Rodberg, Bob Rowthorn, Ian Steedman,
Peter Taylor-Gooby and Alan Wolfe. Since no two of the above
colleagues are likely to agree on its contents, it is perhaps unnecessary
to add that they bear no responsibility for the final product.

Thanks are due to Len Rodberg, formerly of the Institute for
Policy Studies, now at the Public Resource Center, for providing
me with a seven-week visiting fellowship to Washington, DC, in
1977. During this time I was able to discuss my ideas with many
individuals and groups in the eastern United States, all of whose
friendly criticism I much appreciated. I am grateful to Dit Talley
and Susan Stairs for their hospitality whilst I was in Washington,
and to Gordon Forsyth and other colleagues in the department at
Manchester for their co-operation and support in enabling me to go.

Thanks also to all the typists who have wrestled, not always
without complaint, with my shameful handwriting at various stages
in the book's progress; to the secretaries in the department, in
particular Joyce Wolfson; and most of all to Edith Gillett and now

Jean Ashton and all the typists, past and present, of the secretarial reserve.

Lastly my thanks to Sandy and the boys for their support and forbearance. Despite the best intentions, writing a book is always at heart a solitary and selfish process which relies on others more than we care to admit.

To my mother and
the memory of my father

I

INTRODUCTION: WHAT IS POLITICAL ECONOMY? WHAT IS THE WELFARE STATE?

Social legislation and the social services are an integral feature of modern life. The twentieth century, and in particular the period since the Second World War, can fairly be described as the era of the 'welfare state'. Table 1.1 (taken from a recent book by Mishra[1]) speaks for itself. Nor is the welfare state a particularly British institution. Public responsibility in the areas of health, education and social security has mushroomed since the war in every country of the advanced capitalist world, and is reflected in the growing share of GNP devoted to the social services—see Table 5.2, p. 79.

All this is by now well known. Why, then, another book on the welfare state? The reason is that in my view most current writing in the field embodies an erroneous *interpretation* of and *explanation* of the welfare state. For some, such as Crosland, the welfare state along with other features of modern society marks the end of capitalism and its replacement with a different and better society, whether the mixed economy, 'post-industrial' society, 'welfare' society or whatever. For almost all writers within the tradition of social administration and its equivalents abroad, the welfare state has as its goals the satisfaction of human needs and the improvement of human welfare. Consider the following definitions:

[The object of the social services] is the improvement of the condition of life of the individual. (R. Titmuss)[2]

Social policy addresses itself to a whole range of needs—material, cultural, emotional—outside the wide realm of satisfactions which can conveniently be left to the market. (F. Lafitte)[3]

TABLE 1.1   *State welfare in Britain (c.1860 and c.1970)*

	c.1860	*c.1970*
Income security	None (except for Poor Law Relief, as in other services)	Old age, invalidity and survivors' pensions; sickness, maternity and work injury and unemployment benefits (virtually universal scheme). Universal family allowances; national assistance
Medical care	None with the exception of lunatic asylums, vaccination and environmental health services	Comprehensive and free health care for the whole population
Education	None with the exception of educational grant (Parliamentary) to religious bodies	Free and compulsory ten-year education; secondary and higher education with maintenance grants
Housing	None	Over one-quarter of all housing publicly provided, largely at subsidised rent; rent regulation in private sector
Proportion of national income spent on state welfare	1–1.5 per cent	24 per cent

The distinctive feature [of welfare activities] is that their manifest purpose is to influence differential 'command over resources' according to some criteria of need. (J. Carrier and I. Kendall)[4]

Common to all is the view that the purpose of the welfare state is the enhancement of human welfare, the imposition of more enlightened values over those embodied in the capitalist market system. This is normally illustrated by counterposing a policy of *laissez-faire,* assumed to be universal in the nineteenth century, to that of the modern, interventionist welfare state.

This book adopts a fundamentally different approach by treating the welfare state as a constituent feature of modern *capitalist* societies. To do this it utilises a radically different theoretical approach: that of Marxist political economy[5] (about which more later). This situates the welfare state within its contemporary environment: the capitalist economy and its attendant social relations. As a result our approach is both widened and narrowed. Widened because we must treat social policy within its total social context. Narrowed because we consider only capitalist societies and have nothing to say about social policy in the Soviet Union and other non-capitalist countries; nor about pre-capitalist welfare provision in Western countries; nor, for rather different reasons, about social policy in the Third World. Our focus is on the welfare states of advanced capitalist countries.

Immediately, however, we encounter a problem, for the very term 'the welfare state' reveals the ideological nature of most writing about it. Put another way, the object of our study is defined in terms of a theoretical tradition which we reject. Nevertheless, the phrase has entered our language and for the moment we must continue to use it. Nor is the conception of the modern state using its political power to modify the play of market forces[6] entirely a misleading or erroneous one, as we argue below. In Chapter 3 a new definition of the welfare state is presented, but in the meantime we face the problem of defining what it is we wish to study.

For the moment we assume that the welfare state comprises two sets of state activities.

(i) State provision of social services to individuals or families in particular circumstances or contingencies: basically social security, health, social welfare, education and training, and housing. These may be further subdivided into benefits in cash and services in kind. The former refer to money payments by the state with which goods and services can subsequently be purchased—for example, pensions or educational grants. The latter refer to those activities of the state where it directly produces a service 'in kind' which is available free or at a greatly subsidised price—for example, NHS benefits,

education or social work. These all share the characteristic of being 'human' services, which Stevenson defines as an interaction between the provider and consumer with the aim of changing the physical, mental or emotional state of the consumer.[7] This should immediately alert us to the fact that the 'service' may be compulsory and that the 'consumer' may not look upon it as a benefit at all. So much is evident in the case of prison or probation services, but all social services, we shall argue, combine elements of *control* and service *provision*. As Pinker accurately puts it: 'social services are used to impose sanctions as well as to confer benefits.'[8]

(ii) State regulation of private activities (of individuals and corporate bodies) which directly alter the immediate conditions of life of individuals and groups within the population. Again we say 'alter' and not 'improve': the effect can be both quantitative and qualitative, and for 'better' or 'worse' according to some measure of human need. Such regulation would include taxation policies and a whole range of social legislation from the Factory Acts to modern consumer protection, from building by-laws to the statutory compulsion on children to receive education.

This provisional definition of welfare-state activities thus includes a whole range of state interventions above and beyond the direct provision of social benefits and services. On the other hand it focuses attention solely on the state (both central and local) as the agency of intervention. In a celebrated article, Titmuss[9] pointed out that a range of means were available for implementing social policy. In particular he distinguished two 'systems of welfare' apart from the social services themselves: *fiscal* welfare, whereby 'social' goals are pursued through the tax system, and *occupational* welfare, whereby business enterprises directly provide a range of benefits for their labour force, such as health clinics or occupational pensions. Whilst fiscal welfare is clearly included within our definition, the second is not insofar as 'enterprise welfare' develops entirely independently of state action. Now this clearly poses problems if, for example, we wish to understand the 'welfare system' of Japan, where corporations provide a wide range of services elsewhere provided by public agencies. However, the ubiquitous tendency, I would assert, is for the occupational system to become more and more integrated within the public system, so that the state increasingly intervenes in, sets limits on and generally regulates the operation of enterprise welfare. This is certainly so in the case of occupational pensions here and abroad. The result is that the welfare state, as we have defined it, is an ubiquitous feature of all advanced capitalist countries, albeit with immense differences still persisting between them.

POLITICAL ECONOMY AND MARXISM

What is meant by Marxist political economy and how does it tackle the analysis of the welfare state? The whole book constitutes an answer to the second question, but some preliminary words are required on the first.

'Political economy' traditionally refers to the school of classical British economists, notably Adam Smith and David Ricardo. In their major works—*The Wealth of Nations* (1776) and *Principles of Political Economy* (1817)—they developed an analysis of the burgeoning economic system of their day, capitalism. This is characterised, in part, by the generalisation of commodity production, that is the production of almost all goods and services for sale, not for the consumption of the producer. In order to understand the economic and social relations within such a society they developed the labour theory of value, which relates the values of all commodities to their underlying objective cost in terms of human labour. This body of thought was one of the constituents which Marx later incorporated in his analysis of capitalist society. But his major work *Capital* (1867) is subtitled *A Critique of Political Economy* for good reason: he did not simply utilise the concepts of classical political economy in a new way; instead he reformulated the concepts themselves. Nevertheless, classical political economy is rightly seen as one of the intellectual progenitors of Marxism, alongside (according to Lenin) German philosophy and French socialism.

The result of Marx's intellectual work was a completely new social theory, usually known as 'historical materialism'. This term accurately expresses the links and breaks between classical political economy and Marxism. It is 'materialist' because it explains the social world in terms of the interaction of human beings and inanimate nature in the process of producing goods to meet their material needs. Thus Marx's emphasis on the labour process and production, and his development, from political economy, of the labour theory of value and the notion of distinct classes emerging in the economic process. It is 'historical' because, unlike classical political economy, capitalist society is understood and analysed as one stage in a process of historical development. To this end Marx developed the entirely new concept of a mode of production, of which capitalism was one in a succession of different modes. The political economists, he demonstrated, treated commodity production as an eternal facet of human societies, or at any rate as the end-point of a prior process of development. For this reason Marx's critique of political economy is much broader in scope than political economy itself: it provides a theory of history, of social formations and of social revolution.

Not surprisingly this particular offspring of political economy was decidedly unwelcome to the dominant capitalist class of the time, and it is from this date that quite different social sciences replaced the unified field of political economy. Shaw expresses this, rather dramatically, as follows:

> The political economists, with the labour theory of value, had come within a hair's breadth of grasping that economic relations between commodities were based on social relations between classes in the process of production. Marx developed their arguments, and turned them against them, showing the full revolutionary implications of the labour theory of value.[10]

At the beginning of the epoch of imperialism, with the collapse of the belief in inevitable social progress, such a theory posed problems to those in authority. Indeed, Marxism was becoming, and was to remain, the dominant theory of revolution.

At this time Economics and Sociology were born. Making a very broad generalisation, one could say that the analysis of economic relations (People and Nature: Production) was divorced from that of social relations between people. Consequently economics developed by abstracting its analysis from social relations and from specific social structures. Its basic postulates were seen to be as applicable to Robinson Crusoe on his desert island as to the activities of General Motors. At the same time that economics became abstracted from the concrete social relations and social structures of capitalist society, sociology developed a theory of these divorced from the analysis of the central economic problem of all societies—that of production. To quote Shaw again:

Economists after Marx gradually turned away altogether from the [labour] theory and from all recognition of the social character of economics . . . The other side of this decline . . . is precisely the rise of sociology to deal with what economics cannot deal with—the social relations between classes, in their political, trade union, ideological and cultural aspects—without dealing with their real basis in the capitalist mode of production.[11]

It is for this reason that the recent critique of economics and sociology has gone hand in hand with a revival of political economy. This is the relevance of Marxist political economy to an understanding of the welfare state: why, paradoxically, we return to a theoretical approach developed in the nineteenth century to analyse a specifically twentieth-century phenomenon. Marxist political economy *refuses* the compartmentalisation of current social science and seeks to *re-fuse* what have become separate studies of a single phenomenon.

This theoretical apartheid has fatally weakened our understanding of the welfare state. In another article,[12] I distinguish three groups of theories on the welfare state, which draw in turn on sociology, economics and political science, and develop a critique of each. These are:

 (i) functionalist theories of the welfare state;
 (ii) economic theories of government policy; and
(iii) pluralist theories of policy-making.

The first group includes both citizenship and 'technological' explanations of the development of welfare policy, as represented by Marshall, and Wilensky and Lebeaux[13] amongst others. The second consists of applications of welfare economics and the writings of economic 'Liberals' such as Friedman, together with some macroeconomic studies of social spending.[14] The third group includes case studies of social-policy formation as represented by Hall *et al.*[15]

Each of these theoretical traditions have certain strengths and merits. Marshall reveals a central paradox of capitalism: the rights of citizenship are compatible with and developed alongside it, they are 'the foundation of equality on which the structure of inequality could be built'. The industrialisation school stresses the impact of the industrial revolution and its continuing aftermath, though in a partial and one-sided manner, and the impact of the 'dominant elite' in the early phase of industrial development. Macro-economics alerts our attention to the growing conscious control over the blind play of market forces; pluralism to the existence of choice and conflict over social policies. But all contain a parallel series of inadequacies and errors. To spotlight these we may group the theories into two broad types: functionalist and action theories.

Functionalist theories of the welfare state objectify all processes within society and see policy developments as a passive response to these social or non-social 'forces'. There is no room here for humans as active, initiating groups helping to shape their own history. Functionalism does have the advantage that it focuses on the objective social determinants of human history—on laws of development which operate independent of people's consciousness and intentions. It also conceives of history as a *process* and at the same time as *progress*, whether towards greater rationality, goodness or control over the inanimate world. In this, of course, it bears a resemblance to historical materialism and Marxist historiography (and to that of non-Marxists such as E. H. Carr).[16] But, for Marx, the development of the forces of production under capitalism (which he stressed and indeed praised) was precisely one side only of a contradiction with the social relations of production under capitalism (which he just as consistently condemned). To concentrate only on the first aspect, as functionalism does especially in the hands of the 'technological determinists', is to ignore the fact that history is also a succession of qualitatively distinct modes of production, and hence ignores the role of classes, class conflict and revolutionary rupture in human history. Applied to the explanation of the welfare state, functionalist theory recognises its role in producing the type of individual required by 'modern industrial society', but it cannot perceive this type as specific to capitalist society, and hence ignores the welfare state's role as a controlling, repressive agency.

Welfare economics and pluralism have a common ancestor in liberal political theory.[17] This is one reason for treating them together here, but there are two other related reasons. First, they both utilise an individualist methodology which, unlike functionalism, views individuals as the basic units of society and which studies their behaviour in certain situations. The second reason for treating welfare economics and pluralism together is that both schools are 'action-oriented' and embrace the general principles of action theory. That is, analysis is in terms of human subjects—their interpretation of reality in light of their values and their responses to it. Thus explanations of social policy focus on the subjective interpretation of what constitutes a social problem, rather than on the objective determination of the problem as with functionalist theory. They have the merit of stressing the subjective content of human action, the creative role of people in history. They can also accommodate conflict as a determinant of policy, albeit in a limited form divorced from the structural position of classes in society. In these respects they too have something in common with Marxism, but without any conception of structural determination.

Thus, the one school of social science objectifies history, the other subjectifies it. Returning to our original goal—a theory of the development of social policies and of the phenomenon of the welfare state—each performs a partial role. One feature of the contemporary welfare state in an international perspective is the juxtaposition of convergent trends and diverse structures (this point is elaborated in more detail in Chapter 4). Functionalist theories can explain the former—the historic growth of social expenditure and the trend for social policies in advanced capitalist countries gradually to converge. But it cannot satisfactorily explain the immense diversity of social policies which any comparative survey will reveal. *Per contra*, theories of the second school (economic and pluralist theories) can explain this diversity but offer no reason as to why the growth of welfare expenditure and convergence of welfare policies has taken place.

This dilemma is one of the reasons for the continuing strength of the more empirical, eclectic, multi-disciplinary approach of social administration in Britain and its equivalents elsewhere. In the hands of someone like Titmuss it can appear to resolve some of these problems, especially when applied to a particular area of social policy (for example, the health service) or a particular period of history in a single country (social policy during the Second World War). This is not the place to dissect the distinctive features of Titmuss' analysis of welfare policy, but suffice it to note that at various times it has included elements of technical determinism, class conflict, pluralist group analysis and a Durkheimian view of social policy as an integrative element in modern society.[18] But these are all juxtaposed in the corpus of his work in an unsystematic way, such that no theoretical synthesis has emerged despite the great insights to be found in his writing.[19]

My conclusion is, then, that existing theories of the welfare state are fatally weakened by their insistence on either the objective or the subjective element in understanding human history in general and welfare developments in particular. Consequently, neither can adequately grasp their interrelation in the historical process. The only satisfactory resolution to this dilemma, I believe, is that indicated by Marx and encapsulated in his dictum: 'Men make their own history . . . but not under circumstances chosen by themselves.' Of course this does no more than suggest a fruitful approach to the problem. The rest of this book is an attempt to justify this claim by returning to Marxist political economy—the study of the capitalist mode of production—and applying this to our object of study—the welfare states of the advanced capitalist world.

The aim of this book, then, is to provide an analysis of the welfare state under capitalism utilising the theory and methods of Marxist political economy. This description is deliberate. It is *Marxist* political economy because it is founded on the premises of historical materialism. There are other variants within the current revival of political economy, and there are many other thinkers who, whilst critical of orthodox social science, have developed outside this tradition altogether (J. K. Galbraith springs to mind): on the whole they are not considered here. But this is not to say that we apply a fixed doctrine handed down from Marx like the Holy Tablets and exclude all other work. Historical materialism provides a broad paradigm within which different schools flourish and contend. No doubt my particular leanings will emerge in the course of this book.

Second, it is Marxist *political economy* because our study is essentially concerned with the relationship between the economy—the way production is organised—and the political and social institutions and processes of society. In particular we consider the relationship between the capitalist mode of production and the set of institutions and processes that we call the welfare state. I am aware that this particular focus leaves out of account the tremendously important role of ideas and values in the production of social policies. The relationship between the mode of production and the structure of ideas, or the ideology of a society, is a complex one, though materialist theory gives a determining weight to the former in the production of the latter. The political economy approach developed here urgently needs complementing with a study of the ideology of the welfare state.[20] In the process it is unlikely that the major arguments of this book would emerge unscathed, but I believe that the political economy of the welfare state provides the necessary foundations on which a more all-embracing theory of the welfare state can be built.[21]

THE CONTRADICTIONS OF THE WELFARE STATE

A friend once remarked to me that radical attitudes to the welfare state were self-contradictory. In the 1960s, radicals and Marxists were analysing the welfare state as a repressive mechanism of social control: social work, the schools, housing departments, the probation service, social-security agencies—all were seen as means of controlling and/or adapting rebellious and non-conforming groups in society to the needs of capitalism. Yet in the 1970s, he remarked, these self-same people were rushing to defend the welfare state against 'the cuts' and other attacks on it! Now to a certain extent this represents differences of view within the radical perspective on the welfare state; in other words it was not necessarily the self-same group of people acting at both times. But aside from this fact, there is no doubt that he put his finger on the central ambivalence in left-wing attitudes towards state welfare: agency of repression, or a system for enlarging human needs and mitigating the rigours of the free-market economy? An aid to capital accumulation and profits or a 'social wage' to be defended and enlarged like the money in your pay packet? Capitalist fraud or working-class victory?

The position advanced here is that it contains at any one time elements of both. In other words it is not the Marxist analysis of the welfare state that is contradictory, but the welfare state itself. The welfare state exhibits positive and negative features within a contradictory unity. It inevitably reflects the root contradiction of capitalist society: that between the *forces of production* and the *relations of production*, emphasised by Corrigan and Leonard in a previous book in this series.[22] What do we mean by this?

Writing on the impact of modern machinery, Marx describes how, on the one hand, it shatters the traditional division of labour, extends people's control over nature, creates a need for the more rounded development of the worker; yet under capitalism it actually increases insecurity, reduces the individual's control over the labour process, fragments this process and increases the division of labour.[23] Apropos this, Geras comments:

> These pairs of facts are actually contradictions. As such, they represent tendencies which are neither simply progressive, nor simply regressive, because *contradictory*. The essence which explains them, and deprives them of all appearance of contingency, is the central contradiction between forces of production, the increasing productive power of social labour on the one hand, and relations of production, the continued private appropriation of surplus-value, on the other. They partake of this central contradiction and, as partial facts, are only properly comprehended in relation to the social totality which they and it inhabit.[24]

Exactly the same comments apply to the welfare state. It simultaneously embodies tendencies to enhance social welfare, to develop the powers of individuals, to exert social control over the blind play of market forces; and tendencies to repress and control people, to adapt them to the requirements of the capitalist economy. Each tendency will generate counter-tendencies in the opposite direction; indeed, this is precisely why we refer to it as a contradictory process through time.

The roots of this contradiction within the welfare state, though expressed within the state and the spheres of politics and ideology, lie within the capitalist mode of production. This is a way of organising production whereby all individuals are subject to inanimate market forces: what Marx called 'the law of value'. As a result the dominant class within it acts as though it is motivated by a basic drive to maximise profits, and in the process is compelled to accumulate capital. It thus differs utterly from an economic system which serves to meet human needs, yet this is exactly where many orthodox studies of social policy begin and end.

Let us suppose for the moment that a benevolent state existed within a capitalist society and that it attempted to develop a set of policies to enhance welfare, motivated by the desire to meet human needs. It is easy to demonstrate that such policies will soon encounter the constraints of the capitalist economic system. Consider social security for example. If the state were to provide a higher minimum income to eliminate poverty, it would very soon surpass the wages paid to low-paid workers and would act as a disincentive to people to work. It would substantially interfere with the free operation of the labour market. One solution to this might be to replace economic choice by administrative persuasion and coercion, but this would conflict with the intentions of a more welfare-oriented policy. Nor is this all. If the higher minimum income were to be provided on a selective, means-tested basis, either the 'marginal taxation rate' (the rate at which benefit is reduced as income increases) would have to be very high, resulting in the 'poverty trap' and the collapse of the work ethic, or the total cost would be extraordinarily high, in which case the problems of financing this would lead to higher inflation, slower economic growth, or both. If the benevolent state, perplexed by these unforeseen problems, tried to raise minimum wages directly, it would find the competitiveness of the economy eroded and/or unemployment and inflation rising. Twist and turn as it may, the state cannot escape the constraints imposed by its situation within the capitalist mode of production. The welfare state is in a Catch-22 position.

The lesson of this example, which is of course a highly topical area of debate today, can be multiplied in all areas of social policy. An education policy designed to meet the needs of children, however they are defined, will sooner or later come face to face with the unwelcome reality of the labour market and of the uncreative, degrading nature of much modern work. A policy to beautify our cities and plan the physical environment will encounter not only a nest of private property rights, but behind these the blind forces of the urban land and property market, and behind these the free movement of capital between regions and even countries.

However, these examples are in practice misleading, for they assume that the state can be isolated from the capitalist system and can effectively challenge its priorities. A further distinction of a radical approach is that it rejects the notion of the state as a free-floating subject, and substitutes in its place a view of the state as the creature of a particular mode of production.

This implies that the state tends to function so as to secure the conditions for reproducing that mode and the relations of exploitation within it, which under capitalism crucially involves ensuring the continued accumulation of capital. Now in its more extreme version this Marxist approach generates an opposite series of errors to those of orthodox analyses: the state, and thus the welfare state, can only act in the interests of capital and the capitalist class. But this is to forget the necessary concomitant of the class domination thesis, that of class conflict. The working class and other subordinate classes will oppose this domination and exert pressure both within the economy, for example by pressing for higher wages, and within the state, for example by pressing for more welfare. Insofar as this is in any way successful, the welfare state will embody a rationale that also counters that of the market. In some sense it will act to 'meet needs' and extend rights and in so doing will contradict the simple direct requirements of the capitalist economic system. Yet in the process, the environment of capitalism and the nature of the state itself distorts and weakens this aspect of its role.

This then is the reason why we characterise the welfare state as a contradictory phenomenon. To concentrate solely on its 'positive' aspect, as do almost all writers in the tradition of social administration, for example, is to lose sight of its repressive, capital-oriented side. But equally to concentrate solely on its 'negative' aspect, as do certain critical theorists, is to lose sight of the very real gains that a century of conflict has won. The National Health Service, comprehensive social security, and the like do represent very important steps forward and do in part 'enhance welfare'. Yet their structure and mode of operation provide further means for preserving existing exploitative social relations within our society.

Given the universal growth of the welfare state in advanced capitalist countries, a second contradiction has now developed. The very scale of state expenditure on the social services has become a fetter on the process of capital accumulation and economic growth itself. If capitalism more and more engenders a welfare state, it is also proving difficult for capitalism to cope with the problems of financing the requisite expenditure. This was reflected in attempts to reduce welfare expenditure in many countries in the mid-1970s amidst a growing world economic crisis. But again both aspects of the process must be simultaneously comprehended. Advanced capitalist countries both require but cannot afford a growing level of state intervention in the welfare fields. The process of capital accumulation generates new barriers to that very process: in a nutshell, the process is a contradictory one.

This book focuses on these two major contradictions of advanced welfare states: the continual conflict between classes (at the most general level between capital and labour) over the *goals* and *forms* of social policies; and the contradictory process through time as the growth of the welfare state contributes to new forms of crisis (economic, political and ideological) within these societies.

THE PLAN OF THIS BOOK

This book falls roughly into two halves, each focusing in turn on the two basic contradictions of the welfare state noted above. Chapter 2 introduces the basic concepts of Marxist political economy, utilises these to analyse the capitalist mode of production and discusses some of the implications of its development for social policy. In Chapter 3 we introduce the state and relate its growing range of activities and functions to the development of the capitalist economy. Chapter 4 complements this by discussing and theorising how in practice the modern welfare state has developed, in terms of class conflict and its interpretation and mediation by the state. It concludes with a more detailed examination of the post-war period which sets the stage for the remainder of the book.

Chapters 5, 6 and 7 then consider the implications for the capitalist mode of production of this novel area of state activity. In Chapter 5 we chart the growth of welfare expenditure, analyse its causes and discuss some of its political and administrative consequences. This leads on to a detailed study of its impact on the 'social wage', and on profitability, accumulation and growth in Chapter 6. Finally, in Chapter 7 we consider the link between the modern welfare state and the current crisis, and spell out the implications of our analysis for likely future developments in social policy.

Inevitably, the scope of the book is extremely broad. As we have argued, Marxist political economy rejects the traditional distinctions between the orthodox social sciences—economics, politics, sociology and so on—and provides a theoretical framework within which these divisions can hopefully be overcome. Moreover, an approach that focuses on the links between the capitalist mode and social policy must necessarily be comparative in scope, explaining the differences and similarities between countries in the Western World. All this inevitably carries the danger of unwarranted generalisation and a level of analysis too abstract to bear on the specific concerns of people working within or studying the social services. Wherever possible, concrete examples are given to illustrate the points made.

Ultimately, however, one can only hope that the gains from synthesis outweigh the loss of detail in analysis.

Another difficult problem concerns the divergent aims and interests of potential readers of the book. The series is addressed to practitioners in, and students of, social work and the social services. Beyond those there are general social-science students, economists and the general reader, all of whom may have some interest in its contents. Clearly there is a danger of writing for everyone and pleasing no-one. Ideally the book should provide a detailed comparative analysis of developments in social policy and a theoretical application of Marxist political economy in order to understand and explain these developments. Lack of space prevents both these objectives being realised and in the event the first has been sacrificed. The book can therefore most usefully be read by people with some prior knowledge of the welfare services. On the other hand it assumes no prior knowledge of economic theory, Marxism or political economy, and is intended to provide a basic introduction to the latter for all students approaching the subject for the first time. At the same time some of the arguments of the book are contentious and raise issues still the subject of controversy among specialists in the field (this particularly applies to Chapters 3, 6 and 7). To help clarify my arguments at certain points I have developed them in appendices to which interested readers can refer.

2

THE CAPITALIST ECONOMY

We begin with the capitalist economy. The aim of this chapter is to present as simply as possible some basic propositions of historical materialism and Marxist political economy in order to lay the basis for our subsequent analysis of the welfare state under capitalism. Though much of this is not original, current problems and debates will not be shirked, and I shall try to make my position clear. We begin by looking at the basic concepts of exploitation and class and then move on to consider the capitalist mode of production. This permits us to analyse the dynamics of the economic system under capitalism, which in turn forms the basis for our investigation of its implication for social policy. We look here at the way capitalist development creates new 'requirements' for state intervention in the welfare field. This is only a starting point, however, for it does not follow that these requirements will necessarily be translated into social legislation and social provision. This is a much larger question which we tackle in Chapters 3 and 4. Nevertheless our starting point is not accidental and it determines the route we must travel.

EXPLOITATION AND CLASS[1]

The concepts of class conflict distinguish most Marxist writing on the state and the contemporary welfare state from most contemporary social science. Yet non-Marxists such as Dahrendorf[2] also utilise the concepts, though in a very different way, so that it is important to set out clearly our approach to these questions.

Classes are groups of people sharing a common relationship to the means of production. In any class-divided society (that is, all societies since primitive communal societies to the present) there will be two basic and antagonistic classes: those who own and those who do not own the vital means of production (the basic material prerequisites for production). The classes are antagonistic because the former can exploit the latter. Now the concept of exploitation has a precise, scientific meaning in Marx, though this does not mean that it is not also a critical notion. Exploitation refers to the process whereby the former, the *dominant* class, extracts surplus labour from the latter, the *subordinate* class. That is, the total labour of the latter class produces a social product, part, and only part, of which is returned to, or retained by, that class in the form of consumption goods (food, shelter, clothing, fuel etc.). The remainder is appropriated by the dominant class whose members or agents may use it for a variety of purposes: enlarging the stock of means of production, building lavish temples, churches or mansions, engaging in luxury consumption, furnishing large armies or whatever. The total labour time devoted to providing the necessary consumption goods (not necessarily at biological subsistence level) for the producers—the subordinate class—is termed *necessary* labour; the remainder is termed *surplus* labour, and the goods and services it provides for the dominant class is termed the *surplus product*.

At this point it is important to add a little precision to the above and introduce another concept: the mode of production. This refers to the way production is organised and the means by which the production and extraction of the surplus labour or surplus product takes place. On this basis Marx began an analysis of the two great anterior modes of production to the capitalist (at least in Europe): the slave and the feudal. In the slave mode of production, basic productive activity is undertaken by a class without rights or freedom, whose very bodies are owned by their masters. In the feudal mode of production, in return for specific 'obligations' of the lord, the serf must provide so many days' labour services (or their equivalent in cash or kind) to his lord. In both modes, the extraction of surplus labour from the direct producer is direct and obvious; not so in the capitalist mode, considered below. But in all (class) modes of production, for exploitation to take place, two conditions must be met. First, the productivity of labour must exceed the minimum level necessary to maintain life and necessary health and the reproduction of the population. In other words, if productive techniques are so primitive that they provide only the bare subsistence for the direct producers, then there is no material possibility for an exploiting class to exist. Second, one class must own and control at least part of the means of production and thereby be in a position to claim the product of the surplus labour.

These two conditions make it clear that the mode of production refers both to the organisation of the labour process and to the social relations between classes in this process. Put another way, the mode of production refers to the 'structured unity' of the *forces* of production and the *relations* of production.

The mode of production—the way in which one class extracts surplus labour from another—ultimately determines the nature of the entire social structure. This is the core of Marxist historical materialism and it distinguishes Marxist from all other theories of history. Since it is so central and since it is so often misunderstood, it will be worth our while to reproduce a passage from Marx's *Capital* where this is clearly spelt out.

> The specific economic form, in which unpaid surplus labour is pumped out of direct producers, determines the relationship of rulers and ruled, as it grows directly out of production itself and, in turn, reacts upon it as a determining element. Upon this, however, is founded the entire foundation of the economic community which grows up out of the production relations themselves, thereby simultaneously its specific political form. It is always the direct relationship of the owners of the conditions of production to the direct producers—a relation always naturally corresponding to a definite stage in the development of methods of labour and thereby its social productivity—which reveals the innermost secret, the hidden basis of the entire social structure, and with it the political form of the relation of sovereignty and dependence, in short, the corresponding specific form of the state.[3]

From our point of view, the important conclusion is that the form of the state—its nature, structure and role—will be constrained by the mode of production or the nature of exploitation in that society. So too will the 'welfare' functions of that state.

Classes then are groups in antagonistic relation to the means of production within a specific mode of production. One class is the exploiter, the other the exploited. Corresponding to these classes are specific class interests which inevitably conflict and which result in class conflict as an unbiquitous feature of all exploitative societies. However, all concrete societies (or social formations) comprise, usually, more than one mode of production. Hence the class structure of any society will be more complex than this simple dual model for any mode of production, since there will exist classes belonging to other modes. Furthermore, in the capitalist mode of production, important differentiations have occurred within the class of wage and salary workers, for example the well-known division between working class and middle class. (This is considered further below.) However, a particular social formation consists of several modes of production in systematic relation to one another, in which one mode is dominant. So we refer, for example, to modern France as a capitalist society despite the persistence of a significant peasant class within it. The classes of the dominant mode leave their stamp on all classes within it, and the class conflict particular to that mode dominates other forms of class conflict. Hence, in modern capitalist societies, the conflict between capital and labour is predominant. This is especially true of a country like Britain where the capitalist mode has developed furthest and all but eliminated other modes.[4]

THE CAPITALIST MODE OF PRODUCTION[5]

Within the framework of historical materialism adumbrated above, Marx spent much of his life studying the particular mode of production—capitalism—whose development has dominated the past two centuries. The three volumes of *Capital* are the results of this theoretical work. Again, no more than an outline sketch can be presented here. We can best approach this by considering, in the next two sections, his answers to two central questions. How does exploitation take place under capitalism? What are the 'laws of motion' of capitalist society?

Under capitalism most goods and services are produced as commodities, that is they are produced for sale. The product of a factory worker, or even a farmer, is not consumed by the direct producer. It is offered for sale, exchanged for money, and this money is used to purchase other goods. Now this picture of a commodity-producing society would apply to one where every family produced goods for sale; that is, where there are no distinct classes. This is usually referred to as 'simple commodity production'. Capitalism is much more than this—it is one where a class of capitalists owns the land machinery etc., necessary for production and employs workers to operate it. Here the capitalist lays out money to purchase capital goods, raw materials and labour, and at the end of the production process sells the proceeds, recoups his money and makes a profit. The other side of the coin is precisely a class of people who necessarily have to work for the capitalist in order to earn wages to buy their consumption goods. They are not *forced* to work for the capitalist, as the serf is for his lord or the slave for his master. Nor is the remuneration for which they work laid down by religion or administrative fiat. The labour market is a sphere of free exchange between worker and capitalist, yet at the end of the day a profit has been produced which is appropriated by the capitalist. How does this come about?

In order to explain this, Marx took over and reinterpreted the labour theory of value developed by classical political economy, in particular by Adam Smith and David Ricardo. This begins with the observation that, under simple commodity production, the average price of a good (that is, omitting fluctuations due to changes in demand) will be proportional to the labour time taken to produce it. This average, or 'socially necessary', labour time is termed its *value*. So the capitalist under these conditions will purchase machinery, materials and labour at their values, sell the final product at its value and recoup *surplus value* as a result. The question now becomes: where does the surplus value originate? The answer lies in the nature of the particular commodity 'labour'. As we have noted, capitalism is distinct from simple commodity production in that one class—the working class—owns nothing (in the way of productive goods) except its ability to work, or its *labour power*. It is this commodity labour power which it sells to the capitalists, each day or week or month, in return for a wage or salary. Strictly speaking, the worker does not sell his labour, but his ability to labour, or labour power, for a specific period of time.

Now what determines the value of labour power and hence average wages? Marx tackled this by assuming that, like all other commodities, its value is the socially necessary labour time to 'produce' the 'output', in this case the worker. That is the labour time necessary to produce the food, housing, clothing, fuel and any other consumption goods and services required to maintain the worker and his capacity to work. It is immediately obvious, however, that the commodity 'labour power' is a rather unusual one in several respects. First, it is not 'produced' in the way that any other commodity is. Children are reared and adults live their lives in families wherein the population is reproduced. So the value of labour power must suffice, not only to 'produce' the worker, but also to *reproduce* the next generation of workers, the future working class. In the case of the nuclear family, which has been the basic family form under capitalism, it must cover the consumption of children and non-employed wives. Second, the level of consumption of the family, and hence the value of labour power, is not a fixed amount given by biological or other factors. Marx realised this and noted that the value of labour power was determined by 'historical and moral' factors, that it varied between countries and between different periods of time. More importantly, it would also be influenced by the degree of class struggle between workers and capitalists. Thus there is an essential flexibility in the value of this crucial commodity. We shall see that the role of the welfare state is closely related to the problems of reproducing labour power and of determining its value.

The capitalist firm, then, purchases various commodity inputs, including labour power, at their values and sets them to work in the productive process to produce commodity outputs. Here the labour power becomes active concrete labour, whether that of operatives, labourers, technicians, clerks or whatever. The secret of exploitation lies in the fact that this particular 'commodity', unlike all the others, can produce a value greater than its own.[6] That is, in a day or a week it can produce a value greater than the value of the goods and services it consumes in order to produce and reproduce itself. All other inputs, whether machinery or raw materials, can only transfer their value to the final output. But in the case of labour this is not so: it can be compelled to produce an extra value over and above that necessary to produce itself. This extra value is termed surplus value and it is this which is appropriated by the capitalist because he owns the means of production and has purchased the labour power as well. The origin of exploitation under the capitalist mode of production lies, first, in the difference between the value of labour power and the value produced by the worker and, second, in the appropriation of this surplus value by the capitalist firm.

As soon as we move away from a situation of simple commodity production, the one-to-one correspondence between values (that is, socially necessary labour time) and average prices disappears, and the economic models become more complicated. We shall not venture any further here, but suffice it to note that a systematic relation persists between the value categories (values, value of labour power and surplus value) and the real-world phenomena of prices, wages and profits. For example, profits will be larger the greater the amount of surplus value produced. A further complication arises from the obvious fact that the wages of workers differ, as do the values of their output measured in money terms. But again this can be explained in terms of the labour theory of value. At the most abstract level a more educated or trained worker 'costs' more to produce, so that the value of his/her labour power is raised by the labour time of his/her teachers, supervisors etc. Under certain assumptions, however, such a worker will also produce an output of a higher value, so that the rate of exploitation of different workers has a tendency to be equalised. Again, the state plays an important role in fitting the labour force for productive activity in this way.

In this manner Marx demonstrated that exploitation can exist under the capitalist mode of production despite all appearances to the contrary. Despite the 'freedom' of workers to sell or not sell their labour power, and the 'equality' of the market where every good or service exchanges with its equivalent, yet one class can extract and appropriate the surplus labour of another class. One reason for this is the contrast, to which Marx drew attention, between the freedom and equality of the sphere of exchange, and the coercion and inequality of the sphere of production. Once the worker becomes an employee of a particular firm he is at its behest and, within limits, must do as he is told. This applies as much to senior executives as to the lowest paid menial worker. It is in the productive sphere that the relations between capital and labour appear in their most naked form. A second reason is that the 'freedom' and "equality' of the sphere of exchange is itself partly illusory. The worker is compelled to sell his labour power to capitalist firms by economic necessity; the alternative is starvation, the workhouse or a life on social security. Nevertheless the gulf between the first and the last alternative is obvious, and here too the welfare state interposes itself in a crucial way within the capitalist mode of production.

Thus, just as under feudalism or slavery, capitalism is characterised by exploitation and, therefore, by the existence of two fundamentally opposed and conflicting classes. However, our argument so far has done no more than demonstrate that surplus value *can* be produced within the capitalist mode. It has not shown that this will necessarily occur in practice. This problem is raised by the very existence of class conflict. In a nutshell, what is to prevent workers banding together in unions and driving up the value of labour power of real wages until it wipes out surplus value or profit? What mechanism ensures that a sufficient gap always remains between the value of labour power and the value produced? At one level, the domination of capital within the sphere of production provides an answer. Capital can attempt to offset rising wages by raising the level of direct exploitation, for example by extending the hours of work or the intensity of work. These methods were intensively used by capital during the nineteenth century. However, there is a physiological limit to the extent these methods can be used (and it was often reached at this time), so that profitability could not be guaranteed by this method. More important, class struggle also inevitably develops within the productive process. Associations of workers form to dispute the capitalist control over the labour process and to attempt to influence the use made of labour power, the introduction of new techniques etc. Again, profitability cannot be guaranteed nor, therefore, can the continuance of capitalist production. Other mechanisms must also be at work. Marx's answers to these problems constitute the heart of his dynamic theory of capitalist society and form the foundation of his analysis of the laws of motion of capitalism.

Before turning to these, however, I must mention one further factor of great importance, not least in a study of the welfare state; the existence of ideology. This refers to the set of ideas about a society generated by that society. All societies generate a set of beliefs and concepts about themselves which are contradictory. At one level the leading ideas correspond to the reality of that mode of production, yet at another level they are distorted because they present that particular mode of production as eternal. The false appearance generated by ideologies stems from their failure to explain history as a succession of qualitatively different modes of production. Thus much writing by economists on exchange or by sociologists on industrial society assumes the present forms of capitalist society. Sometimes this is contrasted to a previous 'simple' or 'primitive' stage of history, but there is no perception of capitalism itself as a historically specific stage.

But above and beyond this, Marx developed a powerful theory of the particular form in which ideology was generated under capitalism, which he called 'commodity fetishism'. Capitalism presents itself to its participants automatically in a distorted or 'fetishised' way. The sale of labour power takes the form of an exchange of equivalents whereby wages correspond to the value contributed by labour; profits appear as the contribution of capital, and rent as the contribution of land. Furthermore, the existence of classes is hidden by the individualisation of all operations within the capitalist market. The disquiet at collective action, whether by workers or welfare clients, today reflects the way this jars with the dominant ideology of capitalism as one of free and equal exchange between individuals. Finally, as we shall see below, the political process, with its rights of citizenship and individual ballots, also masks the class structure of capitalist society. Just as the arena of exchange hides the sphere of coercion within the economy (the production sphere), so political democracy masks the sphere of coercion within the policy (the armed forces and the repressive organs of the state). Yet so long as capitalism is perceived as the natural order of things, these ideas and explanations of society will appear not only as obvious and inevitable but also, in their essential features, as just. The ideology of the welfare state is a good example here: it distorts the real relationship between capitalism and collective provision, but it is not entirely illusory: it is based on a real foundation.

THE LAWS OF MOTION OF CAPITALISM

The surplus product or, in its capitalist form, surplus value provides the wherewithal for extra means of production (new factories, machinery, transport and other infrastructure). It is thus the *sine qua non* for the renewed accumulation of capital. Yet we have not so far discovered a convincing mechanism which ensures that surplus value will continue to be produced. Does not capitalism beget its own Frankenstein—the modern working class—which can raise wages and eliminate surplus value, thereby bringing the system to a standstill? The mechanism which has so far prevented this from occurring (though not necessarily for ever) Marx called the 'industrial reserve army'. The industrial reserve army consists of not only the unemployed but also marginal groups like the disabled, the seasonally employed, those displaced from previous modes of production (like peasants), immigrants from other countries and, especially important today, housewives. This reserve army of labour exerts downward pressure on wages and prevents the value of labour power rising to absorb the whole of surplus value. Once more we can discern the relevance of many current welfare policies for this process. But once again a further question is posed. What prevents the very accumulation of capital from exhausting this reservoir of labour? We appear to be in a Catch-22 situation: without surplus value no accumulation, but with accumulation no surplus value. The Marxist answer to this conundrum also provides the basis for understanding the peculiar and relentless dynamic of capitalism.

In a nutshell, the reserve army of labour is continually replenished, Marx argued, by the introduction of new labour-saving technology. The more real wages rise, the greater the incentive for capitalists to substitute capital for labour in the productive process. Capitalism, once it has reached the stage of 'modern industry', creates its own means for renewing the supply of labour and thus the basis for accumulation. Unlike the earliest stage in the development of capital, for example the 'putting-out' system in eighteenth-century Lancashire, capital has here seized control of the labour process itself.[7] As a consequence, science is increasingly harnessed in production, and modern technology is born. The industrial revolution, once under way, had a dynamic of its own: the unparalleled development of technology over the past 200 years is witness to that. But its origin and its *raison d'être* is the need continually to recreate the industrial reserve army in order to preserve and extend surplus value and hence permit capital to accumulate.

Once any individual capital has introduced newer cost-reducing machinery or equipment, a second mechanism—competition—ensures that other capitalist firms will sooner or later copy it (or improve on it) on pain of extinction. Capitalism is always characterised by competition between many different capitals so that the laws of supply and demand are a ubiquitous feature of the system, even after the emergence of monopoly capitalism. The recent spread of giant multinational corporations has extended this competition to a world scale, but has not altered its basic mechanism. It is pressure on labour supplies and hence falling profits which provides the stimulus to introduce labour-saving technology. Competition then provides a secondary stimulus to generalise new production techniques as quickly as possible.

The crucial point is that both these mechanisms are peculiar to capitalism. What is usually referred to as the Industrial Revolution of the late eighteenth and early nineteenth centuries, and the era of 'modern industrial society' ever since then, is the product of three defining characteristics of capitalism.[8] These are:

(*i*) the separation of the direct producers from the means of production; that is, a mass working class selling its labour power as a commodity;

(*ii*) the institution of private property in the form of many competing units of capital;

(*iii*) capitalist control over the production process (or labour process) itself and hence over the forces of technology.

Once given these conditions, the dynamic to accumulate capital was unleashed upon an unsuspecting world.

Let us now look at the major dynamic tendencies of capitalism of interest to our study.

First, there is the never-ending development of what Marx called the 'forces of production'. The 'forces of production' refer not only to technology and the means of production, but also the character and organisation of the labour process. This means that they include the nature and structure of the 'direct producers' themselves—the modern working class in its broadest sense. It is apparent that today the adaptation of the workforce, of labour power, to the needs of capitalism is an important part of its development, with many implications for social policy.

Second, as accumulation proceeds, so capital becomes more and more concentrated in larger units—both of ownership (the giant corporation) and of production (the giant factory or office complex). Larger units of production necessitate larger units of control, and of finance in order to fund the enormous capital costs associated with newer technology. The tendencies towards ever-greater concentration and centralisation of capital are among the most prescient of Marx's predictions (writing as he was in the mid-nineteenth century). The growth of multinational corporations spanning the globe represent the latest stage of this process.

Thirdly, the very dynamism of the capitalist mode of production dissolves all previous modes of production within society. Peasant agriculture is undercut by modern capital-intensive agriculture;

the self-employed, whether craftsmen or local shopkeepers, are progressively displaced by factory-produced goods and super-markets; the traditional professions like law and accountancy are increasingly employed within large corporations rather than in small independent firms. The result is that a larger share of the labour force is proletarianised: more and more become employees of someone else, dependent for their living on selling their labour power. This is not to say, of course, that all class distinctions are being eradicated. In this fundamental economic sense there *is* a tendency for the class structure increasingly to polarise into two camps of Capital and Labour, the latter comprising the vast majority of the population. But in another sense new class structures emerge: the traditional petty bourgeoisie declines irretrievably, but a new middle class of technicians, professionals and administrators rapidly develops. How to analyse the new middle classes is still the subject of considerable controversy. Whilst their economic position more and more approximates that of the 'traditional' working class, their position within hierarchies of authority in firms or the state means that political and cultural elements also intervene in determining their class position. Unfortunately, we cannot pursue this question here.[9]

Mention has just been made of modes of production or sectors that are displaced and dissolved by the spread of capitalist relations. However, other sectors of the economy, whilst not part of the capitalist mode as defined, can persist or expand within a capitalist society. One such sector is the state itself of which the welfare state is a part. Much of the rest of this book will be concerned with the precise way that the state sector relates to the dominant capitalist sector. Another example of equal importance to a study of the welfare state is the domestic sector, that is, the family. The way the family develops and its functions change is also ultimately related to the development of the capitalist mode (see Chapter 3 below).

Just as capitalism dissolves anterior modes of production within any given society, so it does on a world scale. Capitalism creates, for the first time in history, a world-wide economic system. Its dynamism, the restless urge to accumulate and expand, and the continual growth in the productive forces which it generates, has meant that all other economic systems have fallen before its advance. This is most graphically seen of course in the development of

imperialism in the last quarter of the nineteenth century, when the
leading capitalist powers divided up the entire remaining surface of
the globe for their colonies. This has misled some into thinking
that capitalism established its sway by armed forces alone, but in
a more fundamental sense it was the 'law of value', or market
forces, which broke down previous modes of production across the
globe. Indian spinners were ultimately displaced not by armed force
but by the inexorable economic pressure of competition from more
productive, lower cost capitalist industry. Colonialism was used
to 'open up' these markets to capitalist competition and to protect
them against depredations from other imperialist countries. In this
way then a *world* capitalist system was established in the late nineteenth century. Note that this too impinges directly on many aspects
of the welfare state. To take one example, since the war millions of
migrant workers have been drawn to the industrial centres of
Europe, so that now one in seven of all manual workers are
immigrants.[10] Their presence graphically illustrates the fact that
capitalism can only be understood as a world system.

The development of the productive forces, concentration of
capital, dissolution of previous modes of production and the
establishment of a world economic system: these are all the results
of the impetus of capital accumulation. The crucial point to note
is that all are the unplanned result of a system which has its own
autonomy and dynamic. Individual persons, whether capitalists or
workers, are pressed by the 'dull compulsion of economic forces'
to undertake actions which result in the tendencies noted above.
Nobody can escape them whilst the system (and it is a world system)
lasts. The secret of capitalism is that *nobody* plans it, as the early
political economists grasped. This is not to say that the intentions
of people have no effect on its history, nor that states, for example,
cannot modify the play of market forces. They can. But equally
they cannot usurp them whilst the capitalist mode of production
persists.

The foregoing presents a picture of capitalism developing in a
unilinear way from its early competitive era to advanced monopoly
capitalism of today. On this basis Marxists distinguish the era of
monopoly capitalism, existing on a world scale since the end of the
nineteenth century. The establishment of giant corporations, the
division of the globe between the leading capitalist countries and,
following from these, a heightened level of class conflict within

countries and international conflict on a world scale, all date from this period. This era has also seen the establishment and development of welfare states, so it provides an indispensable backcloth to our study in this book.

Yet the dynamic tendencies of capitalism do not operate in an even way at a global level. In many ways the capitalist mode of production, like acid, dissolves 'local' peculiarities: many aspects of modern life (from language to architecture) are being progressively 'homogenised' under its impact. But the other side of the coin is the unevenness of capitalist development both within and between countries.[11] Capitalism in the modern era is a world system, but it is one comprising a system of distinct nation states. The development of each country proceeds differently because it occupies a distinct place within the developing world economy and is faced with a different international context. Hence, the second, third and fourth countries to industrialise did not imitate the pattern of development of the first—Britain—for the simple and obvious reason that they followed on and had to compete with an entrenched and powerful competitor. For example, the state played a more important role in establishing a framework for private capital in all countries (including the United States) than it did in Britain.[12] Again, larger corporations became more rapidly established in these countries alongside extremely backward sectors (Tsarist Russia provides a good example), whereas Britain, due to its long economic lead, adopted them at a relatively late stage. As a result it would be true to say that in no other country was the period of *laissez-faire* as lasting or as vigorous as in the United Kingdom, and in many it did not exist at all. In this sense the British pattern of capitalist development, far from being the model for all subsequent countries, was quite unique.[13] This, too, is important to bear in mind when analysing the welfare state, especially from a British standpoint.

This theory of 'combined' yet 'uneven' development provides a fruitful framework within which to further 'periodise' the last 100 years of monopoly capitalism. Until the outbreak of the First World War, Britain was the number-one world power economically, militarily and politically. Despite this, the late nineteenth century witnessed the development of powerful industrial competitors, notably in the United States and Germany. The response of British capitalism was increasingly to insulate itself from the competition of these dynamic economies by investing in the markets of the British Empire, acquired precisely as a result of its contemporary hegemony. Nevertheless, this world hegemony permitted the establishment of free trade and the development of productive forces on a rapid scale. The First World War changed all this: it seriously weakened all the European combatant nations temporarily whilst strengthening the United States. But the by now deep-rooted structural problems of the British economy meant that its supremacy was also rapidly eroded by the growing economies in Europe. The failed attempt to reestablish the Gold Standard signalled its decline. The United States was not yet in a position to assume the mantle of leading capitalist power and the world sank into protectionism, recession and crisis. Yet still the Empire cushioned the British economy, so that the 1930s were paradoxically an era of rising living standards for the majority amid long-term structural decline, and unemployment and poverty for a minority.[14]

The Second World War ushered in a quite distinct new era, comprising a changed balance of forces on a world scale together with a further decline in Britain's position. The latter was the result of war indebtedness, plus the break-up of Empire with the success of anti-colonial struggles, plus the long-delayed effects of the competitive weakness of British capitalism. The post-war period is the record of the (largely unsuccessful) attempts to cope with this legacy. The changed global relations of power reflected two further developments. First, the expansion and strengthening of the Communist Bloc in Eastern Europe, followed in 1949 by the successful Chinese revolution, severely narrowed the global base for capitalist exploitation. The immediate result was the Cold War and the arms race. Second was the emergence of the United States as the undisputed dominant power of the capitalist world. Following the 'interregnum' of the inter-war years, this was crucial in establishing the preconditions for what turned out to be the long boom of the post-war years. The United States, first, ensured that capitalist relations were re-established in the war-devastated countries of Europe and Japan and, second, laid the basis at Bretton Woods and elsewhere for a stable system of international monetary and trade relations which avoided the inter-war plunge into protectionism. This provided one crucial ingredient in the sustained economic expansion which followed, just as the subsequent challenge to US hegemony was one crucial ingredient in the world slump of the mid-1970s.

These then are the four major periods of British and world history within which the development of the welfare-state systems of the Western World must be situated: the epoch of imperialism before the First World War; the inter-war period; the Second World War, reconstruction and the post-war boom; and finally the new period, ushered in in the 1970s, of faltering accumulation and renewed crisis.[15] Needless to say, the particular experience of each period will differ for each nation state. The lesson of this historical pattern for our study is that one must constantly bear in mind not only the common elements and trends in social policies, but also the distinct national forms of state-welfare intervention.

CAPITALIST DEVELOPMENT AND SOCIAL POLICY

The autonomous dynamic of capitalism provides the starting point for a materialist analysis of the welfare state. The course of capital accumulation continually generates new 'needs' or 'requirements' in the arena of social policy. Of course, when using the term 'needs' here we are not referring to human needs, but to the requirements of the capitalist mode of production at a particular stage of its development. To reiterate: it is only a starting point and no single instance of social policy can be explained simply in terms of such a requirement.

To answer comprehensively the question, what are the implications of developments in the capitalist economy for social policy, would require a book in itself. In this section we simply take four major tendencies at work within the capitalist mode of production and discuss the implications of each for *one* area of social policy. No more than this is intended or attempted.

(i) Proletarianisation and the growth of social security. This clumsy word refers to the tendency for a greater proportion of the labour force to become employees of somebody else, rather than independent, self-employed people. It is a ubiquitous feature of all capitalist economies that the share of wage and salary workers rise, whilst that of the self-employed, whether farmers, artisans, shopkeepers or professionals, declines. Britain was the first country to experience capitalist industrialisation, and this process has developed further here than in any other. By 1960 only 7 per cent of the labour force were employers or self-employed (that is, 93 per cent were paid

employees), compared with 19 per cent in France for example.[16] Whatever the real income level, a 'proletarian' in this sense owns no capital on which to fall back in hard times. Contingencies like old age or sickness leave the working-class family defenceless in a way quite unlike that of, say, a peasant. Furthermore, capitalism generates one unprecedented new contingency—unemployment. Underemployment, seasonal idleness, even casual employment, were known before the industrial revolution, but the lack of any productive activity is a phenomenon peculiar to capitalism.

The very condition of being a paid employee, then, exposes a family to hardship through loss of wage, for whatever reason. The development of modern social-security systems is ultimately grounded in this basic fact.[17] Of course, as we keep repeating, it is not a sufficient explanation, for how could one explain the very different dates at which social security in its modern form originated: in Germany in the 1880s, in Britain in the first decade of the twentieth century, in the United States not until the 1930s? Furthermore, social security has never been a response to a purely technical process of industrialisation. It has always been essential, for example, to maintain an incentive to work and to reinforce the discipline of the factory over the workforce when operating unemployment schemes. For this reason, in all advanced capitalist countries, a worker can be disqualified from receiving unemployment benefit if he/she has left a previous job without 'good' cause', or was sacked for 'misconduct', or refuses to accept an alternative job offer, or is involved in a trade dispute.[18] Ultimately it is adapted to the needs of a capitalist organisation of industry.

(ii) Technological change and legislation on working conditions. The first modern factories were the textile mills of Lancashire at the turn of the nineteenth century, and this marked the limit of what Marx called 'machinofacture', as opposed to manufacture, during the first industrial revolution. It was not until the early twentieth century that factory organisation of the production process developed in certain other industries, such as armaments and chemicals; not until the inter-war period did it become generalised throughout manufacturing industry; and not until the post-war period did it seriously develop within other fields such as distribution and services.[19] The development of a fine division of labour coupled with the increasing use of machinery was not entirely due to its technical superiority, as

Marglin[20] has demonstrated, but due to the need to strengthen capitalist control over the labour process in the face of a rapidly developing working class. Once again the capitalist form of industrialisation left its stamp. Nowhere was this more glaringly apparent than in the conditions of labour within the factory during the early years of the industrial revolution. Hours of work increased to unheard of levels, child labour under inhuman conditions spread, industrial health and safety measures, let alone basic amenities, were non-existent; the relentless and intense nature of the labour too was quite unprecedented.[21]

These developments underlay a series of attempts by the state to control the hours and conditions of work in the interest, amongst others, of ensuring that the workforce was not literally worked to death. Britain was the first to experience the development of the factory and the first to introduce factory legislation, in a series of Acts from 1833 to 1853. These were chiefly concerned with limiting the hours of work of children and women, together with imposing some rudimentary standards on safety and other conditions. Since the factory form predominated in the textile industry, the Acts applied only to this sector. They were later extended to other industries, beginning in 1874 and 1878.[22] Since then the state has progressively intervened here and in other countries to regulate conditions of work. It is notable, for example, that in almost every country the first group to receive social-security benefits were the victims of accidents at work.[23] The Workmen's Compensation Act of 1879 marked the beginning of this process in the United Kingdom.

(iii) The division of labour and the growth of education.[24] Capitalist industrialisation introduced the modern form of the division of labour; not only the broad social division of labour between an increasing range of different crafts and occupations (this had long existed), but the minute fragmentation of activities within the factory. Consequently, this division of labour required two new qualities in the labour force: the appropriate skills and cognitive abilities, and an acceptance of the new disciplines and routines of factory life. The latter was all the more necessary in the face of the erosion of traditional family forms and of traditional belief systems, especially religion. Subsequently the development of the productive forces under capitalism enlarged the range of skills and altered the nature of educational attainments required of the labour force.

The development of modern education systems is in part a response to these trends. Too often this is seen as a steady quantitative extension of knowledge and skills throughout the population in industrialised countries, but this is once again to neglect the capitalist form of the division of labour. For some it has indeed brought about an unheard-of level of education, but for many others it has inaugurated a process of de-skilling—the loss of old skills and their replacement with nothing but an ability to mind machinery.[25]

Furthermore, it requires the qualitative adaptation of labour power to quite new methods and rhythms of work. One result has been a general trend for education to develop in three stages, from *mass* education, through the separation and extension of *secondary* education, to the post-war growth of *higher* education. The 1870 Education Act provided the basis for elementary schools in Britain; in parts of the United States, mass education arrived rather earlier. One aim was to integrate the rapidly growing and newly enfranchised proletariat by providing the necessary socialisation (in America it also served to integrate the flood of new immigrants into American nationhood). Consequently the schooling emphasised the learning of particular functions, the inculcation of authority and discipline.

The progressive development of technology, new industries and a growing white-collar workforce necessitated the second stage—the emergence of a separate system of secondary education, initially for a minority and later on for all children. In Britain, Balfour's 1902 Education Act laid the basis for this development, though it did not become widespread until after the 1944 Education Act: even by 1938 only three-quarters of 12–14-year-olds were at school and only one-fifth of these received tuition in separate secondary schools.[26] Secondary education in the United States developed earlier so that, by 1930, 29 per cent of 17-year-olds received education. This ultimately reflects the earlier and more thorough development of the monopoly capitalist stage in America. New methods of control were also required over the growing white-collar salariat, where direct measures of output and productivity and direct control over work are less possible than with manual labour. 'Progressive' education and IQ testing, both pioneered at this time, provided a means of internalising work norms and securing co-operation from the new middle classes.

The third stage—the growth of higher education—reflects the

characteristics of advanced capitalism, and so again there is a different chronology between the two countries. At the end of the Second World War, one-fifth of 18–21-year-olds in the United States were enrolled in higher education, and the present proportion is about one-half. In the United Kingdom, expansion did not really get under-way until the Robbins Report of 1963. Nevertheless the common trends are unmistakable and are related to the further transformations of the social divisions of labour: the massive growth of demand for technically and other highly qualified labour and the increasing proletarianisation of this labour. The former has required a growing level of education for part of the school population; the latter the increasing specialisation and fragmentation of their knowledge. It is for this reason that the expansion of higher education has doomed the traditional liberal arts approach of the old universities in all advanced capitalist countries.

(iv) Urbanisation and urban legislation. Another major trend accompanying capitalist development is urbanisation. Population grew rapidly in nineteenth-century Britain, almost quadrupling in just over a century, but the urban population grew more rapidly still from 30 to 80 per cent of the total. It is true that London was a large city at the beginning of this period: this, plus its role as capital city, meant that a series of unique problems developed here in the nineteenth century.[27] But other towns and cities developed rapidly, so that by 1901 over 13 million people lived in just six conurbations, a peak percentage of 43 per cent of the population. Britain is now the most urbanised of the major capitalist countries, but the trends charted here are universal and have their roots in the capitalist mode of production. According to Raymond Williams:

> Capitalism as a mode of production, is the basic process of most of what we know as the history of country and city. . . . The division and opposition of city and country, industry and agriculture, in their modern forms are the critical culmination of the division and specialisation of labour which, though it did not begin with capitalism, was developed under it to an extraordinary and transforming degree.[28]

Large cities have existed throughout the history of civilisation, but urban living as the norm is a specific product of capitalism.

'The city is as necessary to capitalist reproduction as the factory is to capitalist production.'[29]

The rapid growth of industrial cities has prompted the need for controls over activities within urban areas and subsequently the direct provision by the state of infrastructure, housing and other amenities. Necessarily, Britain was here too an unwilling pioneer, though (just as in the field of factory legislation) it was for a long time partial, permissive and unenforced. Throughout the nineteenth century it took the form of a maze of acts concerning public health, sanitation, vaccination, nuisance legislation and local government reform, primarily concentrated in the period between the 1848 and 1875 Public Health Acts.[30] More positive legislations on town planning did not begin until the 1909 Housing and Town Planning Act, and substantial provision of state housing not until after the First World War. But the relentless dynamic of capitalism lets nothing rest. Since the Second World War the operation of the property market has, despite some controls, transformed numerous towns and cities. Housing areas in city centres have been removed to make way for commercial office development, housing has become more dispersed and segregated into either private or council house developments, whilst industrial production has become more mobile. The emergence of the 'corporate city' in the United States[31] suggests there are similar trends at work in all modern capitalist countries, though responses to these have varied enormously, as a comparison of town planning policies in Britain and the United States demonstrates. These new trends lead to further requirements on the part of capital for state provision, such as transport networks suitable for a more dispersed population and employment structure.

This chapter has presented an analysis of the capitalist economy as an unplanned system with its own in-built 'dynamo'. The last section has considered a few of the developmental tendencies at work as a result of this and sketched out some implications of these for social policy. One implication that could be drawn is that the mode of production generates certain functional requirements in the field of welfare policy which the state or some other body outside the economy must necessarily perform.[32] This is emphatically not the position taken here. It *is* useful and helpful to analyse the changing functional requirements of capitalist economies as we have done, but it does *not* follow that the state will necessarily perform those functions. Before we can understand whether, and to what extent, it does so, we must consider two further questions. First, what is the link between the state and the capitalist economy, and how are the requirements of capital mediated by the state. Second, what is the role of class conflict in determining social legislation and provision. These two questions form the subject matter of our next two chapters.

3

THE STATE AND ITS
'WELFARE' ACTIVITIES

What is the nature of the state in capitalist society? Is it a neutral mechanism for reconciling conflicting interests and for representing the 'common interests' of the nation, as pluralist political theory would have it? Or is it, in the famous phrase of *The Communist Manifesto*, 'but a committee for managing the common affairs of the whole bourgeoisie'? The common element in all Marxist theories of the state, which distinguishes them from all other theories, is the subordination of the state to the particular mode of production and to the dominant class or classes within that mode. In other words, the *economically* dominant class is also the *politically* dominant or *ruling* class. Nevertheless, reality is a good deal more complicated than this bald phrase of Marx and Engels would suggest. In particular there is in Marx's writings, in contrast to those of Engels and Lenin for example, a much richer analysis of just what is specific about the *capitalist* state, which is after all the object of our study here.[1] What follows is an outline of what I consider to be the most relevant points in this theory for understanding the welfare state. In recent years a wide-ranging debate on these issues has occurred, and those interested in some of the underlying theories, and my own position, are referred to Appendix A at the end of this book.

The analysis of capitalism developed in Chapter 2 uncovered two specific features not found in previous modes of production. First, exploitation takes place automatically within the economic system; that is, the extraction of surplus labour does not require the political coercion, open or latent, of feudalism or slavery. The generation of surplus value is secured without conscious control by means of the market. Second, and due to this, the capitalist economy has a momentum or dynamic of its own which is again basically outside the control of any agent or class. Together these indicate that under capitalism the 'economy' becomes separated from politics, the 'private' sphere from the 'public'. The notion of a distinct political sphere is, therefore, peculiar to capitalism. The very individualism of capitalism, the fact that all subjects are formally free and equal to pursue their own ends, requires a separate structure, the state, to represent their 'common interest'. What results are the separate institutions of the modern state and their apparent autonomy from the relations of exploitation.[2] It is this appearance which permits most students of the welfare state to counterpose the rights of citizens or the needs of people, as mediated by the state, to the requirements of the market. This appearance is not entirely false, but it is only a partial truth.

What Marx demonstrates in this way is that the very existence of political freedom is a necessary condition for exploitation to take place. The latter is based on the free sale and purchase of labour power as a commodity. For exploitation to take place all that is necessary is that capitalists (who own the means of production) and workers (who do not) should be treated identically before the law as free and equal partners. Any feudal or other ties on the free sale of labour power are anathema to capitalism and must be removed for capitalist relations to be established and reproduce themselves. Paradoxically, the capitalist system demands freedom and equality before the law in order for exploitation to take place. In Marshall's words, the growth of citizenship provides 'the foundations of equality on which the structure of inequality could be built'. Rather, we would say that capitalist exploitation and inequality provided the foundation on which the structure of political 'freedom' and 'equality' can be built.

This also helps us understand the persistence of representative democracy and modern Parliaments within the advanced capitalist world this century, despite intervening periods of fascism and military dictatorship in certain countries. One reason for this is that representative democracy corresponds particularly well to the 'free' and 'equal' treatment of individuals as individuals which is necessary for capitalist exploitation to take place.[3]

In its turn, representative democracy becomes a most powerful ideology (grounded in reality), consisting of a belief by the population that they 'exercise ultimate self-determination' through the state. The reasons for the spread of liberal democracy in the Western World lie beyond its functional congruence with capitalism (they are touched on in Chapter 4). Nevertheless, modern legislatures are specific to the capitalist mode of production.

Ultimately, however, this requirement of political equality and freedom is a paradox, for ultimately the rule of any class rests on force. This means that a distinct instrument of coercion is also required. Alongside the legislature we find the armed forces, the police force and the judicial systems of modern states. It is true that since all class societies rest on some form of coercion, these 'repressive state apparatuses' are common to all, but only under capitalism do they become separated from the economically dominant classes and centralised in the separate institutions of the state. Lastly, for reasons discussed in subsequent chapters, the executive and administrative branches of the state have grown tremendously in recent years. Their power has increased not only absolutely but also relative to that of the legislature. Parliament is but one part of the ramifying state system of modern times.

To summarise, the capitalist state takes the form of a set of institutions, consisting of the repressive apparatus, the judiciary, the legislature, the executive and the administrative branches, together with local and regional organs of government and increasingly a range of *ad hoc* semi-public bodies. These all have in common their separation and relative autonomy from the economic 'base'—the capitalist economy. But we now appear to have moved a long way from our starting point—that this self-same state acts to secure the political domination of one class by another. By what means does this state apparatus serve the interests of the dominant capitalist class and secure the conditions for the reproduction and accumulation of capital? This is still the subject of considerable debate, referred to in Appendix A, and only a brief answer to this important question can be given here.

The first point to note is that the state requires a degree of autonomy from the economically dominant class(es) in order adequately to represent their interests. As Miliband points out, 'the *common* affairs of the *whole* bourgeoisie'[4], implies that there are different and potentially conflicting elements within this class, and that they have sectional as well as common interests. If the state is to act as more than a sounding board for these various pressures, if it is to act in the long-term political interests of the capitalist class as a whole, then it must clearly be distinct and possess a degree of autonomy from this class. Only in this way can it perform such a reconciling and mediating function. It is not the only institution performing this function—the political parties based on the capitalist class, independent foundations and 'think-tanks' and so forth also play their role—but it is by far the most important institution today.

However, this still leaves open the question why the state *should* act in this way, rather than reflect impartially the interests of all groups in society as pluralist theories of the political process would have it. In answer to this question, Miliband puts forward three distinct explanations. The first concerns the personnel of the state:

> The people who are located in the commanding heights of the state, in the executive, administrative, judicial, repressive and legislative branches, have tended to belong to the same class or classes which have dominated the other strategic heights of the society, notably the economic and the cultural ones.[5]

They therefore share certain common ideological and political positions, values and perspectives. The second answer concerns the power which the capitalist class can wield over the state

> by virtue of its ownership and control of economic resources and of its strength and influence as a pressure group, in a broad meaning of the term.[6]

This focuses on the imbalance of class power in capitalist society. The third explanation is in terms of the 'structural constraints' which its insertion within the capitalist mode of production imposes on the state. Whatever the class background of state personnel, or the pressures exerted on the state from outside, the capitalist economy

> has its own rationality to which any government or state must sooner or later submit, and usually sooner.[7]

These are all important factors, but it may be deduced from the foregoing that in my view the third is the most important. The class background of state personnel can change. The class power of capital can be partially countered by the class power of labour. Yet in a country like Britain, where both these factors are important, there is little indication of any fundamental change in the state, or of the welfare state for that matter.

But the third explanation is relatively empty if the nature of these 'structural constraints' cannot be specified. Here it is crucial to remember that we are dealing not with one all-powerful world state, but with a system of nation states of varying power. The historic origins of this go back to the era of absolutist states within Europe, a product of the long decline of feudalism. But once capitalism became established on a world scale, the sovereign nation state became generalised as the norm. At the same time, as we have seen, capitalism continued, and continues, to develop an ever more integrated world economic system. The 'law of value' or market pressures now operate on a global scale: the rise of multi-national corporations is a reflection rather than a cause of this movement. It follows that any single nation state cannot entirely ignore the requirements of capital accumulation and reproduction. To do so would invite the flight of capital to other, more promising, centres of accumulation. This is one major reason why the nation state, short of a revolutionary change, will not contravene the long-run imperatives of capital accumulation.

But this requires in turn that the majority of the population accept this domination of capital, and here the ideology of the modern state is all-important. The state is regarded as the representative of the common interests of 'a people', precisely because it is premised on the individual interests of capitalist society. Because the general or social will is abstracted from the genuine interests of individuals, the state paradoxically sanctions or legitimises the latter.

> In the name of a universal principle (the obligatory aspect of 'law' as expression of a general or social will) it consecrates private property, or the right of individuals to pursue their own exclusive interests independently of, and sometimes *against*, society itself.[8]

This process in capitalist societies provides a powerful ideology buttressing every operation of the capitalist state. Its relevance to an understanding of the emergence of citizenship and the welfare state is obvious, but unfortunately we cannot pursue this any further here.

So for these reasons the autonomy and independence of the capitalist state, and *ipso facto* of the welfare state, is only apparent. What distinguishes Marxist theory is not the view that a particular class dominates the institution of the state (though this is the normal state of affairs), but that whoever occupies these positions is constrained by the imperatives of the capital accumulation process. But at the same time the separation and relative autonomy of the state permits numerous reforms to be won, and it in no way acts as the passive tool of one class. Within these constraints there is room for manoeuvre, for competing strategies and policies. There is scope for the various organs of the state to initiate policies, to reverse them, to make choices and to make mistakes. So we reject here both the pluralist view of the state, that it is a neutral arbiter between competing groups in society; and the crude economistic view, that it is but an instrument of the dominant class in society. An analysis based on the *relative* autonomy of the capitalist state avoids both these pitfalls and permits what is hopefully a fruitful understanding of the modern welfare state.

THE WELFARE STATE

This chapter concentrates on the relation of the state and the welfare state to the capitalist mode of production. In this section we develop a theoretical framework for analysing the welfare activities of the modern capitalist state. In the next section this is related to its other activities, and areas of conflict between these sets of activities are investigated. Our approach means that this chapter has a 'static' character: we focus on the *structural* relationship between the state and the economy. The basis for proceeding in this way has been provided in the section above, where it was argued that the capitalist mode of production imposed certain constraints over state policy. But this structural relationship cannot explain the origin and development of any single act of social policy. This requires among other things an analysis of the dynamic tendencies at work in advanced capitalist countries—those inherent in the development of the capitalist economy, outlined in Chapter 2, and the all-important role of class conflicts—and the way these are politically and ideologically mediated within the state. Some of these questions are tackled in Chapter 4, which must necessarily be read in concert with the present one.

What then are the defining features of social policy or the welfare activities of the modern state? For the purposes of this work we shall characterise the welfare state as *the use of state power to modify the reproduction of labour power and to maintain the non-working population in capitalist societies.* The remainder of this section elaborates this approach.

The major means available to the state were discussed in Chapter 1: the direct provision of benefits and services, the parallel use of the taxation system, and state regulation over the private activities of individuals and corporate bodies. The welfare state or social policy does not here refer to benefits with similar characteristics that are provided by other agencies, such as occupational welfare provision, insofar as they are completely independent of state control. However, as we noted in Chapter 1 there has been a continual tendency for the public domain to encroach on the private, and there must be few occupational, charitable or voluntary forms of welfare provision in contemporary Britain, say, that are financially independent of and totally unregulated by the state.

The welfare activities of the modern state, according to our definition, are divided into two: first, the reproduction of labour power. Labour power refers to the capacity of men and women to perform labour; the continual reproduction of this capacity is therefore a necessary condition of all human societies. Under capitalism, two basic mechanisms ensure that this takes place. First, the labour of workers (of all kinds) earns them a wage or salary with which they purchase consumption goods and services: food, housing, clothing, transport, recreation, beer and so forth. The consumption of these use-values continually replenishes the capacity to perform work in any given society and period of time. Secondly, within the family a further set of use-values is produced, mainly by the housewife and mainly in the form of services: shopping, the preparation of food, cleaning, washing clothes and so forth. Without these services the consumption of commodities purchased in the market is difficult or impossible.[9] Together, the consumption of both sets of use-values continually replenishes the capacity to perform labour.

The modern welfare state now intervenes in this process in several ways:

(*i*) First, the amount of money which people have available to spend on consumption goods is altered via the taxation and social-security systems.

(*ii*) Second, the nature of the use-values which they can purchase may be regulated by the state, as when it controls additives to food or the facilities provided in new housing.

(iii) Third, particular goods and services are subsidised, either for some or for all, such as certain categories of housing or types of food.

(iv) And fourth, the state directly provides use-values in the form of services, such as the National Health Service, free or at a greatly reduced cost. Here a third component enters the reproduction of labour power alongside commodities bought on the market and the services of 'domestic labour': collectively produced social services. The capitalist sector, the domestic sector and the state sector thus contribute directly to the reproduction of labour power.

In all these ways the welfare state increasingly controls the level, distribution and pattern of consumption in contemporary capitalist society. (These matters are further developed in Chapter 6.)

But the role of the state in the reproduction of labour power extends beyond these quantitative aspects. The type of labour power required in the 1970s differs from that required in the 1870s. Work in modern capitalist society requires certain kinds of abilities, motivation, self-discipline and so forth. So the reproduction of labour power also involves a qualitative element—specific patterns of socialisation, behaviour, specific capacities and personality structures. Among the social services, education, social work and manpower programmes are perhaps most specifically directed to this end. Family allowances and insurance benefits of various kinds, housing policies and health services are perhaps more concerned with the quantitative aspects.

Furthermore, the reproduction of labour power clearly involves not only daily reproduction but generational reproduction; that is, the rearing and socialisation of children. Here the family and the labour of housewives is still all-important, but again it is increasingly augmented and regulated by the welfare state. Almost all social policies have a bearing on the capacity of the family to bring up children, and many are specifically directed at the minority of families that at any given time are doing so: not only education, but specific health services for example; and within maintenance and housing policies special regard is given to those families with children. Children form the workforce of the next generation and this is one reason for the growth of state intervention in this process. In the rapidly changing society of contemporary capitalism their productive capacities must be adapted to changing requirements, such as the changing division of labour (see Chapter 2). In all these ways the contemporary welfare state modifies the reproduction of labour power within capitalism.

But this does not exhaust its functions, for the population also contains individuals that are not part of the workforce. The second arm of the welfare state serves to maintain non-working groups in society. All societies contain groups that are unable to work for their living (aside from those who, in class societies, do not need to): children, the elderly, the sick and disabled, the mentally handicapped and so forth. Of course the boundaries between working and non-working groups are not fixed; they will predominantly be determined by the prevailing mode of production. The sharp boundaries separating working life from childhood on the one side and old-age retirement on the other are in fact specific to capitalism.

Nevertheless, if we accept that all societies contain non-working individuals, it follows that all societies must develop mechanisms for transferring part of the social product from the direct producers to these groups. Again, family and kinship structures play a key role in this transfer in all societies and even today they continue to do so, beyond as well as within the nuclear family.[10] But this is increasingly being supplanted or regulated by a variety of state measures, and this constitutes the second major area of activity of today's welfare state. Pensions and other social-security benefits are of growing importance in transferring purchasing power to these groups, alongside personal and occupational provision via insurance and superannuation schemes. A variety of health and welfare services provide numerous forms of support in kind for the elderly or the sick, gradually usurping the role of kinship and community in the past, and of charitable and voluntary bodies in the more recent past.

In fact this second role of the welfare state cannot be sharply distinguished from the first, for several reasons. Most important is the fact that children are an unproductive group but one which form the future working population. Here the process of their maintenance becomes fused with that of reproducing future labour power. Moreover, in present-day capitalist society the transfer of resources to this particular dependent group is still basically the responsibility of individual families (though increasingly hedged around by intervention from the state). Secondly, many other non-working groups are still potentially part of the workforce, the working-age sick or unemployed for example, so that the form of transfer required is rather different to that for, say, the chronically sick. In Marxist terms these groups constitute the reserve army of labour, hence their maintenance can also be included under the heading of labour power reproduction.

Nevertheless the two basic activities of the welfare state correspond to two basic activities in all human societies: the reproduction of the working population and the maintenance of the non-working population. The welfare state is the institutional response within advanced capitalist countries to these two requirements of all human societies. However, it is far from being the only social institution to perform this role. As we have noted, the family and wider kinship structures continue to play a part, and a few words are required on the interrelationship between the capitalist mode of production, the family and the welfare state.[11]

The development of the capitalist mode of production has fundamentally altered the structure and functions of the family. Whether or not a true extended family system existed in pre-industrial Britain, it is certain that the family combined within it production and consumption activities. The emergence of capitalist social relations, notably the 'free' labourer, shattered this family form and instituted the present divorce between the 'breadwinner' and the 'housewife': between *production* and *reproduction*. The 'modern' family developed in the nineteenth century amongst the middle classes but its stability among, especially, the lower working classes was always problematic. Here, rapid and uncontrolled urbanisation weakened the traditional social control of both family and community simultaneously. The 'maladaption' of the working-class family became the concern of the Charity Organisation Society in the 1880s, and the practice of social work originated at this time. From this has developed a further set of welfare activities by the state designed to buttress and support the family in its role of reproducing and maintaining the population.

> The Welfare State [writes Wilson] has always been closely connected with the development of the family and has acted to reinforce and support it in various ways.[12]

Specific state policies concerned with the functioning of the family and with relationships inside it have tended to follow the initial provision of an infrastructure of social services. For example, in Britain the social-work profession has burgeoned since the welfare reforms of the 1940s. By this time, however, the family was undergoing further change. The rapid rate of accumulation in the post-war period was drawing more and more women into the labour force and, necessarily, more of these were married women. This raised anew the old conflict between 'women's two roles'—work and family, production and reproduction—especially as the employment rates of young married women were rising most rapidly. At the same time rates of divorce and separation have escalated so that in the United States today 10 per cent of all adult women are divorced or separated. This signals new ways of resolving the conflicting ideals of individual development and mutual dependence within the modern family, but it may also interfere with its role in reproducing and maintaining the population. For example, in modern Britain one million children are now growing up in single-parent families. The post-war contortions of social policy and social-work services for the family reflect the state's attempts to grapple with these unforeseen changes in its role and functioning.

To summarise then, the welfare state denotes state intervention in the process of reproducing labour power and maintaining the non-working population. It represents a new relationship between the state and the family in this process. The dynamic of capital accumulation continually alters both the requirements of capital, particularly with regard to the first, and the capacity of the family to meet these requirements. This approach does not explicitly deal with the ideological role of the welfare state, which is touched on in the next section in the context of discussing the overall 'functions' of the modern state. But it provides, hopefully, a useful starting point for examining the political economy of the welfare state.

THE FUNCTIONS OF THE MODERN STATE

The modern capitalist state impinges on all areas of life. Aside from the field of social policy, it regulates business and commerce, intervenes in the labour market and industrial relations, conducts relations with other states, provides infrastructure services such as transport and communications, directly produces goods and services for sale, and since the Second World War has assumed responsibility for overall economic management. And this is only the beginnings of a list of its activities. Most of this growth in state activity has taken place in the twentieth century, in the era sometimes referred to as 'monopoly capitalism'. The welfare state in its modern form is a product of this era and, in particular, of the period since the Second World War, which we refer to as a distinct period of 'advanced capitalism'.

The era of both monopoly capitalism and the welfare state is often contrasted with an earlier period of *laissez-faire* capitalism, characterised by small-scale capital and a minimal role for the state. This was true for only a very restricted range of countries, and possibly only for the United Kingdom, the leading capitalist country of the nineteenth century. In Italy, Russia and Japan, for example, the role of the state in creating the conditions for capitalist production and in abetting the development of monopoly capital were fused in time around the late nineteenth century: an intervening period of *laissez-faire* was unknown. This greatly affected the pattern of welfare legislation in these countries and served to differentiate it somewhat from the British. As a result, only in the Anglo-Saxon countries is the sharp contrast between *laissez-faire* and the welfare state continually drawn by students of social policy. But once the world economy developed, those countries in a favourable position began or consolidated a period of capitalist expansion and emerged as the dominant Western economies today. So that those countries which now comprise the advanced capitalist world have followed a roughly similar sequence since the end of the nineteenth century. During this period the role of the state has mushroomed and the modern welfare state has been forged.

How are we to classify this maze of activities and what relation do they bear to the welfare activities analysed above? These are the questions discussed in this section. In the process we shall look at some recent Marxist work on the functions of the modern state. Now in Chapter 1, functionalist theories of the welfare state were criticised as 'objectifying' social processes.

Implicit in any discussion of the state's functions is the assumption that the analysis tells us something about the determinants of state action, that the state responds to the functional requirements of capital. This is quite unjustified. The fact that some function is required for the accumulation or reproduction of capital (like the reproduction of labour power) tells us nothing about whether or not the state meets those requirements or the manner in which it

responds to them.[13] This involves a study of the way these requirements are translated into political demands and policies—the subject
matter of the next chapter. However, whilst we must reject any
functionalist explanation of the welfare state, it is still useful to
delineate the functions of the state, so long as they are used to
indicate tendencies at work within the capitalist state. This follows
from our earlier analysis of the autonomous dynamic of the capitalist
mode of production and the constraints which this continually
imposes on state policies.

The most important Marxist work in this area in recent years is
The Fiscal Crisis of the State by James O'Connor.[14] O'Connor discerns
'two basic and often contradictory functions' that the capitalist state
must try to fulfil: *accumulation* and *legitimisation*.

> The state must try to maintain or create the conditions in which
> profitable capital accumulation is possible. However, the state
> must also try to maintain or create the conditions for social
> harmony.[15]

On this basis he argues that all state expenditures have a twofold
character corresponding to these two functions: *social capital* and
social expenses. Social capital in turn comprises two distinct sets of
activities, *social investment* and *social consumption*, so that altogether
the following three categories of state expenditure are distinguished:

(i) Social investment: projects and services that increase the
productivity of labour.
(ii) Social consumption: projects and services that lower the reproduction costs of labour power.
(iii) Social expenses: projects and services which are required to
maintain social harmony—to fulfil the state's legitimisation function.

The first two (social capital expenditure) are indirectly productive
for private capital; other things being equal, they augment the rate
of profit and accumulation in the economy. Social expenses, on the
other hand, are not even indirectly productive for capital. They
are a necessary but unproductive expense.

He notes that nearly every state agency is involved in both
functions, and that nearly every state expenditure is part social
investment, part social consumption and part social expense.

However, a preponderant set of political—economic forces determines each area of intervention and permits us to classify them accordingly. Turning to the welfare activities of the state, according to O'Connor they consist of all three activities. Some education spending constitutes social investment by raising the productivity of labour; some does not. Social insurance schemes help reproduce the workforce (social consumption) whereas 'income subsidies to the poor help pacify and control the surplus population' (a social expense).[16]

If we return to our original definition of the welfare state, we may now more precisely describe the two categories of welfare activity. State reproduction of labour power refers to the direct public provision of goods and services, or to state action to modify their nature, extent and distribution. All these forms of welfare expenditure comprise social consumption. The maintenance of non-working groups, on the other hand, falls into the category of social expenses. So too might other ideological or coercive activities of the welfare state which have nothing to do with modifying labour power, but are concerned with controlling or adapting in one way or another groups within the population that threaten social stability. This would include the activities of some social workers, community workers and race-relations bodies as well as the more obvious work of police, prison and probation staff. Many social services, of course, fall into both categories, for example social-assistance schemes (in Britain, Supplementary Benefit and Family Income Supplement) and the plethora of youth-training and employment schemes. They have the aim in part of maintaining and adapting the 'reserve army of labour', a potential labour force, and in part of maintaining and controlling groups that threaten social stability. (Appendix B summarises these and other classifications of state activities and develops some of their important economic implications analysed in Chapter 6.)

What is the relevance of this to an understanding of the welfare state? First, it enables us to situate state social policy within the wider framework of state interventions. Social services which help serve the reproduction of labour power are part of a broader set of state activities which also serve this function, for example commuter transport systems and water and sewage systems insofar as they serve the needs of the working population, not industry. (Alternatively, we might redefine the social services of the welfare state to include these services.) Welfare policies that help maintain and control the non-working population are part of a broader set of activities encompassing the police and judiciary.

Second, and more important, it permits us to analyse the conflicts between these functions of the state and their manifestation in conflicts over welfare policies. The contradiction between social investment and social consumption (some would say between accumulation and reproduction functions) may well appear within social policies themselves. Let me give some examples from the field of social security. Economic stabilisation policies since the Second World War have often used social-security taxes and benefits: for instance, unemployment benefit provides a form of automatic stabilising mechanism, rising when aggregate demand in the economy and hence employment levels are low, and falling when they are high. More generally, the fixing of contribution and benefit levels, the distribution of financing between firms and workers, the size of the Exchequer contribution are all determined with economic (accumulation) as well as social (reproduction) goals in mind. But the functions of social-security schemes do not stop here. In Germany, higher pension benefits at earlier ages have been used as an inducement for workers in particular occupations like mining to retire early in order to permit 'rationalisation' of the industry. In Italy, firms in the south pay very much lower social-security contributions as part of the government's regional policies.[17] In Britain, the introduction of redundancy payments in 1964 was expressly linked to the need to reduce the labour force in a number of basic industries: large lump-sum payments would hopefully reduce worker opposition to these moves and permit the 'rationalisation' of these industries. Pension funds play an important role in Britain as a source of finance for industry, real estate, etc. They amount to a form of compulsory savings channelled into a few giant funds and assurance companies. Recent proposals by Benn to harness these sources more purposively for national economic development indicate the growing attempts to fuse 'social' and 'economic' policies.

Thirdly, conflicts continually occur within social policy between the function of reproducing labour power and that of maintaining other groups and securing social harmony. An education system geared to the productive requirement of the economy may not serve the purpose of integrating and socialising the young. Conflicts can occur within health policy between gearing services to the needs of the labour force (a system of industrial health services) and those of non-working groups (a national health system). Housing policies that permit mobility of labour may not secure integrated community structures. Social-insurance schemes for the working population serve different goals, compared with more universalistic schemes designed to maintain non-productive groups, avoid severe deprivation and maintain social harmony. Hence there are endemic conflicts within social policy between the three goals of capital accumulation, reproduction of labour power, and the legitimation of the wider social system. These conflicts are reflected in the conflict over the level and direction of state expenditure, analysed in Chapter 6.

This chapter has developed a framework for understanding the functions of the welfare state under capitalism. From a political economy viewpoint we may distinguish its role in reproducing labour power from that in maintaining the non-working population. In a broader context these activities may be related to the functions of securing accumulation and legitimation. But the *functions* of social policies must always be distinguished from their *origins*. Analysing the former can, strictly speaking, tell us nothing about why a particular policy was enacted, how it was administered, and so on. It is to this all-important question that we must now turn.

4

THE ORIGINS OF THE
WELFARE STATE

THE ORIGINS AND FUNCTIONS OF SOCIAL POLICY

To disentangle the origins and functions of welfare policies let us begin with Marx's own study of the British Factory Acts in the nineteenth century.[1] He demonstrated how the Ten Hours Act and other factory legislation was the result of unremitting struggle by the working class against their exploitation, yet ultimately served the longer-term interests of capital by preventing the over-exploitation and exhaustion of the labour force. The short-term economic interests of each individual capitalist conflicted with their longer-term collective interests:

> Capital takes no account of the health and length of life of the worker, unless society forces it to do so . . . under free competition, the immanent laws of capitalist production confront the individual capitalist as a coercive force external to him.

The outside intervention of the state was necessary to nullify the anonymous pressures of the market on each firm. Yet Marx was clear that this intervention was not initiated by representatives of the capitalist class, indeed it was persistently and fiercely opposed by them: 'The establishment of a normal working day is the result of centuries of struggle between the capitalist and the worker.'[2] Paradoxically then, it would appear that labour indirectly aids the long-term accumulation of capital and strengthens capitalist social relations by struggling for its own interests within the state. One could apply this approach to much welfare policy this century.[3] The core of truth here lies in the fact that the working class is both an element of capital ('variable' capital) *and* a living class of human beings struggling to enlarge their needs and living standards. But this still leaves us with several problems.

This chapter tries to tackle these problems by confronting two particular questions: what is the role of class conflict in explaining the emergence of welfare policies? And how are the 'functional requirements' of the capitalist system mediated by the state? These twin questions arise from the nature of the capitalist state analysed above. It provides the political terrain on which class struggle can be fought and temporarily resolved, and it is also a mechanism for ensuring the accumulation and reproduction of capital and its social relations. This theory of the capitalist state in turn reflects the analysis of the capitalist mode of production developed in Chapter 2. To recap, it has two major characteristics: first, a system of exploitation and therefore endemic class conflict between, at the most general level, capital and labour; and second, an economic system with its own autonomous laws and dynamic. Simplifying greatly we may say that Marxist political economy is a theory which encompasses a 'structural' view of the economy and a conflict theory of class struggle. Mishra writes: 'one of the strengths of the Marxist approach over functionalism is that it combines a "system" analysis (society as an interconnected whole) with a group perspective (social change resulting from conflict of values and interests).'[4]

One might add that it shares this strength over 'pluralist' or 'action' theories too. In other words the dichotomy between these two basic approaches to understanding the welfare state, criticised in Chapter 1, can be overcome within Marxist political economy. It has the merit over pluralist theories of social policy in situating the 'conflict' within an ongoing mode of production, and it has the merit over functionalist theories of social policy in relating the socio-economic 'system' (its structure and its development through time) to the class conflict which is an integral feature of it. Of course, it does not simply sit these two theories side by side: both elements are developed within a completely different theoretical framework adumbrated above.

That said it is still the case that some Marxist studies of the welfare state veer towards one or the other of these two poles. Some writers see the welfare state as a functional response to the needs of capital (whether its economic needs or its political needs to absorb potential unrest and threats to stability); others see the welfare state as the unqualified fruits of working-class struggle, as concessions wrested from an unwilling state.[5] Most, like Saville,[6] for example, stress both aspects of the welfare state, but leave open the way in which they are related. The present chapter attempts to provide a framework for answering this question. It looks at the effect of class conflict on welfare policies, at the way in which the state represents the interests of capital and at the interrelation between these two sets of forces. The last section applies this approach in more detail to the welfare states of the post-war period. Inevitably, the chapter is brief and schematic, and I am only too well aware that each country in each period represents a unique configuration of circumstances. Ultimately, only a thorough comparative historical analysis will do,[7] albeit one situated within this or some similar theoretical framework.

The necessity for this stems from another feature of contemporary welfare states already referred to: the co-existence of similar trends across all countries with immense diversity in national social policies, organisations and structures.

The most striking indication of the convergence of welfare states is the tendency for state expenditure on the social services to rise as a share of national income in every country of the OECD, a feature noted in the first chapter and substantiated in Chapter 5. But this is not all. In numerous areas, welfare *policies* are converging, though it is less easy to document these qualitative changes. In the field of social security a recent OECD report[8] notes the convergence between two groups of countries with very different historical antecedents. One group, consisting of France, Germany and some other continental countries, early on established social-insurance benefits for specific occupational groups. During this century and especially since the war these have been modified in various ways (moving to pay as you go financing and universal coverage) and they have gradually incorporated a national social minimum within their schemes. The second group of countries, primarily Britain and Scandinavia, began in the opposite way by providing national minimum benefits via a combination of insurance and assistance schemes, but have since the war added earnings-related insurance-based benefits to their basic flat-rate schemes. According to the report,[9] the result is that

a convergence can be noted between those countries that had relied on the social insurance principle and which have extended the scope of public aid or social assistance; and those that had relied on more or less flat-rate universal benefits and which have seen moves towards the supplementation of these by earnings-related contributions and benefits; moreover all countries seem to have moved in the direction of more universal effective coverage.

Yet despite these trends, any student of social policy is struck by the immense diversity between different countries. The relative 'backwardness' of the United States (and, in a different way, Japan) in welfare provision has long been recognised. It alone in the Western World has no system of family allowances nor a comprehensive health insurance scheme. In the field of social security, different countries rely to differing extents on income-maintenance programmes versus benefits in kind (such as housing or labour-market policies); on insurance, assistance or universal benefits; on direct state provision versus state regulation of third-party provision; and so on.

A comparative approach is therefore crucial to an understanding of the modern welfare state. The basic pattern, described above, is of convergent trends at work on diverse national patterns of welfare activity.

The result today is a vast complex of programmes, in which the conflict between the forces pushing towards international uniformity and those representing long established traditions and institutions is resolved in a somewhat haphazard manner that defies simple description.[10]

CLASS CONFLICT AND THE GROWTH OF THE WORKING CLASS

The role of pressure from subordinate classes and other organised pressure groups associated with them is of recognised importance in explaining the introduction of welfare measures. Bismarck's social-insurance schemes in the 1880s, Lloyd George's unemployment insurance scheme of 1911, the improvement and extension of Italian social-security benefits in 1969, the introduction of the National Health Service or of comprehensive schooling in Britain, all represent in varying ways the pressure of the working class and allied groups.[11] However, the modes through which class pressure generates welfare reforms are many and various. At one extreme, reforms may be introduced as a direct result of extra-parliamentary mass action, as in France following May 1968 and in Italy following the 'Hot Autumn' of 1969. At the other end of the spectrum, reform may be devised by representatives of the ruling class in the state to forestall the dangerous growth of an independent class movement, and may even be opposed by the subordinate classes (Bismarck's use of social insurance provides the first and classic example of this tactic). We must clearly investigate this phenomenon in a little more detail.

The ultimate source of the contradictions of capitalism is that it generates a mass working class whose interests are fundamentally opposed to those of capital. The growth of large factories and other assemblies of work concentrates the members of this class and this, in conjunction with the increasingly collective nature of their work, develops their abilities to organise and act together. Whilst this collective organisation is almost always focused on the workplace or industry, and on the economic and control issues arising therefrom, it has on occasion become generalised to involve the whole nation in, for example, general strikes. This is aided by the extensive spread of capitalist relations over the last century as more and more groups, including higher professional workers, have become salaried employees.

However, the class structure of advanced capitalist societies is much more complex than this simple dual model suggests. Indeed, on this basis almost the entire population of a country like Britain, apart from the capitalist class and the traditional 'petty bourgeoisie' of the self-employed, would be members of the working class. In fact there are many divisions: there is the 'new' middle class of managers, administrators and others occupying positions in hierarchical organisations, together with technologists and technicians; there is the growing army of state employees; and there are divisions within the manual working class between those in regular employment and what O'Connor calls the 'surplus population'.[12] Unfortunately we cannot develop a sophisticated analysis of this contemporary class structure here. Suffice it to note that many of these intermediate groups (the exception is the disadvantaged substratum at the base of the working class) occupy, in Wright's phrase, a *contradictory* class location.[13] Because they are situated in an intermediate position within the social relations of production, political and ideological factors play an important role in determining their class position. The 'core' working class can be defined as those with no control over labour power, means of production or investment and resources. It thus stands in an antagonistic relation to the capitalist class proper which controls all three, and this defines the fundamental parameters of class conflict in capitalist society. The 'new' middle class and other intermediate groups play some role in this control process and therefore occupy a contradictory position in this class conflict. Hence, the form of economic, political and ideological conflict in any particular society will have different implications for the class position of these groups.

Having said that, the core of the 'labour movement' in all advanced capitalist countries consists of the unionised, predominantly manual, working class. When we refer to class conflict its essential form is between the labour movement and the capitalist class (itself by no means a homogeneous entity).

The next crucial point to make is that class conflict is now partially expressed through the political arena in advanced capitalist countries. Bourgeois democracy, that is, universal suffrage and freedom of political expression and organisation, emerged in the late nineteenth and twentieth centuries to become the normal form of organisation of the advanced capitalist state. As Therborn points out,[14] it was not instituted by any of the original bourgeois revolutions from the seventeenth-century Commonwealth onwards. Instead, it was fought for by the emerging working class in these countries and was long resisted. Even by 1939 only eight countries could be characterised as democratic according to the single criterion of universal suffrage for both women and men, and there are numerous other criteria which must be taken into account. We must therefore distinguish between class conflicts over welfare policies before and after the institution of liberal democracy. During the period in which it was emerging, the struggle for welfare policies related to the struggles for political democracy in a variety of ways. At times the same forces abetted the simultaneous development of both (for example, in Australia and New Zealand in the late nineteenth century); at other times welfare rights were consciously used as an alternative to democratic rights (in Germany in the 1880s). Once universal suffrage and the other major liberal rights are established, this provides a crucial channel through which to obtain welfare improvements. Indeed, welfare becomes a means of integrating the enfranchised working class within the capitalist system and of obtaining certain concessions from the organised labour movement (this is discussed further below and in Chapter 7).

The creation of a proletariat and the relative autonomy of the capitalist state (both inherent features of the development of capitalism) thus brought about liberal democracy in the advanced countries. This was further accompanied by the rapid growth of worker's parties in many countries—that is parties which drew their membership, leadership and electoral base predominantly from the working class. These were the mass social democratic parties before the First World War, of which the German SPD was by far the largest; and since then the labour and social democratic parties together with certain mass communist parties, notably in France and Italy. Before August 1914, all adopted a revolutionary socialist programme, but the outbreak of war saw a major split develop between what became the communist parties and the social democratic parties. The latter, though all espousing a 'socialist' programme, were henceforth defined in opposition to revolutionary socialist parties. (Soon after, of course, the triumph of Stalinism profoundly transformed the communist parties themselves.) But both groups of left parties have today one feature in common: their links with the growing trade union movement. There are important differences between countries; for example, the British Labour Party emerged as the parliamentary mouthpiece of the labour movement and is very much the child of the trade unions, whereas the German SPD developed before the era of mass trade unions. Nevertheless, most social democratic parties have had trade unions directly affiliated to them at some time and this fact demarcates them from other non-left parties.[15]

The growth of mass working-class parties in this way has also exerted pressure on the older parties of the capitalist and petty-bourgeois classes to coalesce. These parties have a longer history dating from the period of bourgeois revolutions (in those countries which saw them). In any case the franchise was everywhere initially confined to the propertied classes, and their parties developed accordingly. But the later growth of working-class parties has generated a tendency towards a two-party system in an increasing number of countries. It is by no means universal yet, with several parties still competing in France for example, but the parallel growth of large Christian Democratic parties and their equivalents on the Continent does represent a tendency towards a simplified two-party system.[16] The particular strengths and divisions between the two 'sides' in the developing class conflict under monopoly capitalism provides a useful framework for understanding the growth of both political and social rights, and hence the welfare state.

THE STRUCTURE OF THE CAPITALIST STATE

Class conflict alone, however, will not suffice to explain the origins and development of the welfare state—if this were all we would be back with a Marxist variant of the pluralist theories criticised in Chapter 1. For there *are* imperatives created by the capitalist industrialisation process, and there *are* functions to be performed which cannot be carried out by individual business firms, as we argued in Chapter 3. Furthermore, there are numerous examples available where social policies have been introduced by the state, in the interests of preserving capitalist relations for example, against the interests of the working class. Or where policies, originally the result of class struggle, are adapted to serve the needs of capital. There are numerous examples where forward-looking representatives of the capitalist class perceive the need for the state to step in and perform 'reproductive' functions. For example, the Edwardian reforms, such as the 1906 School Meals Act, were partly the result of the growing social imperialist ideology among sections of the ruling class: the recognition that an adequately fed and fit working class was an essential weapon in the growing inter-capitalist rivalry— economic, political and military—of that period.[17]

We have then to explain how the long-term interests of the dominant capitalist class are formulated and enacted in the welfare field. Political parties representing the capitalist class undoubtedly play an important role in this process. One of the functions of liberal democracy is to permit alternative programmes and strategies to be aired and decisions to be taken between them. Yet this process too needs to be situated within the confines of the capitalist state structure. On many occasions the state, operating within the constraints of the capitalist mode of production, will act against the wishes, expressed via 'its' political party, of major sections of the capitalist class. In other words the state may override the short-term, sectional interests of particular 'fractions' of capital in order to benefit the longer-term interests of capital as a whole. What we wish to discover is the mechanism by which these more general interests are mediated and articulated by the state.[18]

What this implies and what has increasingly emerged this century is, according to O'Connor, a 'class conscious political directorate' within the state machine.[19] The state is much more than the legislature: it comprises also the executive, the vast complex of government administration (the Civil Service), the judiciary, the military and, below it, the organs of local (and regional) government. Broadly speaking the growth of such a class-conscious political directorate has seen the emergence of the executive and the administrative branch (in Britain, the Cabinet and Civil Service) to prominence over Parliament. The former becomes the institutional seat where the strategic interests of national capital are represented, mediated and formulated. In other words, the ability of the state to act in a cohesive way to represent capitalist interests is undoubtedly reflected in the centralisation of the state system. It is the President in the United States, the Prime Minister's office and the Cabinet in the United Kingdom, which have extended their powers this century, whilst Congress and Parliament have declined in relative importance.

Nevertheless, a comparison of the United States and United Kingdom will prove instructive here, for there are still crucial differences between the state structures in the two countries and these, it will be argued, are also related to their different welfare policies. First there is the obvious fact that the United States is a federal state, and that the separation of powers between President, Congress, and the Supreme Court is enshrined in the Constitution. In Britain, on the other hand, a unitary state (up to now) and Cabinet government ensure a more homogenous form of government. Partly as a consequence, the relative power of Congress *vis-à-vis* the executive is substantially greater in the United States than that of Parliament in the United Kingdom.[20] Furthermore, the administration is much more fragmented in the United States: a plethora of bureaus and federal agencies overlap with the major departments, quasi-judicial bodies and the powerful congressional sub-committees.[21] Add to this the fact that many important positions are appointed by the administration and it is apparent that the United States lacks a homogenous administrative apparatus. By contrast the long-established, career-oriented British Civil Service, together with a powerful Treasury, provides a relatively centralised instrument for formulating and implementing longer-term class-based policies.

One major factor accounting for this difference in state structures is undoubtedly the lack of a previous monarchical absolutist state in the United States. Within the European context, too, the earlier history of different countries helps explain the forms of state structure and hence of welfare interventions. Britain's long experience of world hegemony resulted in the most extreme form of *laissez-faire* state in the nineteenth century. For half a century from 1850 the role of government in internal affairs was minimal. Yet the hegemonic position of the capitalist and landed classes ensured that an alert, class-conscious political directorate was preserved and that a powerful Civil Service evolved during this period.[22] By contrast, in Germany the state introduced capitalism 'from above', given the weakness of the indigenous bourgeoisie. Consequently, when faced with the growth of trade unions and the Marxist SPD in the 1870s, it was in a position to use the resources of the state to head off the new class threat. One result was the sequence of social-insurance schemes covering health (1883), accidents (1884) and old age and invalidity (in 1889).[23] The late development of a capitalist class and the early development of the proletariat fused together the period of centralised absolutist state and modern welfare state in a single, pioneering whole.

Nevertheless this does not provide an entirely convincing explanation of the nature of different state structures, nor of their effects on subsequent welfare policies. In the first place, it does not account for the steady move towards centralisation in all countries this century. And second, there are the apparent anomalies of countries like Australia which also lacked a prior feudal stage, yet which witnessed the early development of class politics and welfare policies. To go further, we need to consider the interaction between the growing working class and the forms of the state.

CLASS STRUGGLE, THE STATE AND SOCIAL POLICY

We have discerned two factors of importance in explaining the growth of the welfare state: the degree of class conflict, and, especially, the strength and form of working-class struggle, and the ability of the capitalist state to formulate and implement policies to secure the long-term reproduction of capitalist social relations.

It is highly likely that the respective importance of each varies over different policy issues. For example, the fact that higher education is most developed in the United States suggests that direct working-class pressure has not been crucial in bringing about the growth of tertiary education since the war. On the other hand, the absence of housing and comprehensive social-assistance policies there, by comparison with Europe, suggests that the introduction of these owes a great deal to the existence of unified labour movements and relatively strong social democratic or communist parties.

Yet in an important third group of cases it would appear that both capital and labour are pressing for extended state intervention in the welfare field, that there is a congruence of interests tending in the direction of developing the welfare state. For example, the introduction of health insurance in 1911, or national insurance in 1948, was supported by representatives of both classes in their major respects. It is a common feature of social legislation that it is supported by different groups for quite distinct or opposed reasons. For example, the Abortion Act in 1967 was favoured by those seeking further liberalisation in many matters relating to personal life, and by those concerned with the 'cycle of poverty' and the reproduction of problem families (some adopting an almost eugenicist stance). This lends support to two erroneous views of social policy. One is the evolutionist view—that the welfare state represents a harmony of interests in society. The other is the view of some Marxists that working-class struggle for welfare reforms always ultimately works in the interest of capital.

Our analysis, however, permits an alternative explanation of this 'coincidence of interests'. Briefly, it is the threat of a powerful working-class movement which galvanises the ruling class to think more cohesively and strategically, and to restructure the state apparatus to this end. Those countries which have experienced strong, centralised challenges to the power of the capitalist class are those which have developed a unified state apparatus to counter those challenges. A recent article expressed this as follows:

Working class struggles which potentially threaten the political domination of capital or the execution of state functions critical to the accumulation of capital necessitate ruling class restructuring of the state to preserve capitalist political domination and to insulate critical functions from working class influence.[24]

This challenge may take a variety of forms: widescale strike activity and the growth of powerful indigenous unions, as in Britain in the years preceding the First World War; a sweeping electoral victory for working-class parties, as after the Second World War; or, in the extreme case, revolutionary insurrection or the threat of it, as in several European countries immediately following the First World War. The responses also differ, but all involve a move towards a more centralised interventionist state. And more generally, the arrival of working-class parties in the Parliamentary arena has brought about the removal of crucial decision-taking activity to the executive and administrative organs of the state.[25]

It is in this context that periods of innovation and growth in welfare policies can be understood. Both of the major classes see these policies as in their interests, but for quite different reasons. The working class because any policy which mitigates hardship or which modifies the blind play of market forces is to be welcomed. The capitalist class because it reduces working-class discontent, provides an added means of integrating and controlling the working class, and offers economic or ideological benefits too. Because underneath it all the interests of capital and labour are opposed, so the apparent harmony of interests rapidly breaks down. This can take the form of myriad conflicts over the nature of the service or the way it is organised (as in education following the 1944 Act), or over the level of benefits and the conditions attached to their receipt (as in social security following 1948), or the respective size of the state sector (as in housing policy in the 1950s), and so on. Underlying all these is a potential conflict over who controls the social services.

The experience of such periods of social reform in turn generates an ideology of the welfare state, one that *is* premised on a harmony of interests. This is especially visible when one considers the whole line of Fabian/social democratic thinking on the welfare state within Britain. The number of leading individuals within that movement who have personally combined 'socialist' with social imperialist or corporatist beliefs is not simply coincidence. Sidney Webb, Wells and Shaw all favoured state-directed activity to eliminate the unfit, and other reactionary 'national efficiency' policies.[26] Oswald Mosley's corporatism found equal room within the Labour Party and the National Movement. In more recent years Aubrey Jones, a leading Conservative industrialist, politician and theorist, could write: 'This irresponsibility [of labour] can be overcome only if labour is made to feel that it has the same purpose as capital, and that while they remain rivals, their rivalry is subordinate to a unity'[27], and then proceed to implement this philosophy as architect of the incomes policy under the 1964–70 Labour Government. The role of labour and social democratic governments in developing the welfare state, as well as the interventionist state, has been a crucial one. It reflects the steady incorporation of the working class, via their trade unions and parties, within advanced capitalist societies, though this very incorporation throws up fresh contradictions with which the rest of this book is concerned.

Piven and Cloward[28] provide an excellent case study of these factors at work in the US Great Society Programme of the 1960s. The explosion of welfare relief that took place during this period and the plethora of new programmes for the cities were, they argue, a response to the unprecedented rioting of blacks in the northern cities from 1964–8. This in turn resulted from the forced immigration of blacks to the cities from the south in the 1940s and 1950s as a result of the rapid and ruthless modernisation of southern agriculture. The rioting and breakdown of law and order saw also the breakdown of the traditional political machines which ran the cities. The result was a series of Presidential initiatives by Johnson in order to quell this by now dangerous threat: the series of programmes from the 1964 Economic Opportunity Act (II) to the 1967 Neighbourhood Service Programme. In each case the Federal Government, and in particular the executive branch, bypassed state and local governments in order to initiate these policies speedily. The aim was to integrate black leaders within the urban political system by providing them with limited resources and decision-making powers (the slogan of 'maximum feasible participation'). In this way many 'agitational elements' were absorbed and the crisis eventually ended.

This case study shows, first, that at a time of national crisis it was the executive of the Federal Government which acted as the 'class-conscious political directorate', bypassing other levels of government. Second, that welfare policies were deliberately used as a 'ransom' (to use Joseph Chamberlain's phrase from another era) to quell a potentially dangerous threat to the American political and economic system. But third, the absence of a strong labour movement supporting the black movement, indeed often hostile to it, meant that the reforms granted were superficial and temporary.

Soon after, under Nixon, the pendulum swung the other way and there were successful attempts to 'reform' welfare by increasing its reactionary social control and work-enforcing features. Finally, the absence of a powerful, centralised and politically represented labour movement in the United States meant that a thorough restructuring of the state apparatus was not necessary, and that in matters of both the centralised state and the welfare state the United States continues to lag behind many other advanced capitalist countries.

At the risk of gross oversimplification and misinterpretation, Figure 4.1 summarises the argument developed in this chapter.[29] It sets out in extremely schematic fashion the factors influencing the development of social policies adumbrated above: (1) working-class struggle and influence; (2) the centralisation of the state; and (3) the influence of the former over the latter discussed in this section. These factors are by no means exhaustive but constitute, I believe, the major determinants of the modern welfare state.

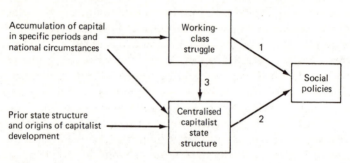

FIGURE 4.1

Of course the ways in which the development of capitalism influences the struggle of the working class and other oppressed groups are very complex. One must take into account the rate of development of the capitalist world economy and its international context, and the place of each country within that world economy. This will also determine the ability of the state to concede the reforms demanded by the labour movement and/or representatives of the capitalist class. For example, the importance of British imperialism up to the Second World War in providing the resources for both the welfare state and personal consumption must not be underestimated. In 1931 Britain's imports could exceed its exports by 6 per cent of its GNP, thanks to the vast inflow of profit and other returns on overseas capital, permitting domestic expenditure to exceed output by a similar amount. This undoubtedly provided an important leeway with which to finance concessions to soften class conflict—a leeway that has now totally evaporated.

The last section looks at the post-war period in a little more detail and tries to apply the analysis developed so far. It also provides a bridge to the rest of the book, which is mainly concerned with the implications of the post-war welfare state for the advanced capitalist world.

ADVANCED CAPITALISM AND THE WELFARE STATE

The post-war world has witnessed two periods of welfare expansion: during the Second World War and its aftermath in the 1940s, and in the period from about the mid-1960s until the mid-1970s (see next chapter). We shall look briefly at the reasons for both, in the advanced capitalist world in general and in Britain in particular.

The end of the Second World War saw a very different world to that which entered it.[30] For the advanced capitalist countries two changes were crucial. The United States emerged as the sole hegemonic capitalist power—dominant in the economic, political and military spheres—whilst Europe and Japan were temporarily crushed. And the Soviet Union too emerged as a world power in possession of the whole of Eastern Europe. The primary aim of United States policy was to secure the stabilisation of Western Europe and Japan and rapidly to reconstruct capitalist relations within these countries. In a series of moves, of which the Marshall Aid plan was the most spectacular, it had achieved these objectives by the end of the 1940s. In this it was considerably assisted to begin with by the left-wing governments then in power in several countries; for example, in Britain the Labour Government rapidly established the Atlantic Alliance as the cornerstone of its policy. Soon after, in fact, there was a series of defeats for the working-class struggles which had brought such governments to power, but their legacy remained.

This legacy was most clearly seen in the greatly expanded role of the state in economic and social policy matters, and in the greater integration of trade-union and working class party leaders within the state. These shifts were welcomed and even encouraged by many political representatives of the capitalist class at that time, for several reasons ably summarised by Panitch:[31]

(i) The necessity of sustaining trade-union co-operation during the course of the war with the promise of continued prominence in decision-making after the war and a commitment not to return to pre-war conditions;

(ii) the recognition that the experience of full employment and comprehensive planning had led to rising expectations of a post-war rise in living standards and security on the part of the working class;

(iii) the example of the Soviet economy (much played up during the wartime alliance) and the concern regarding its effect of the working class in the post-war period;

(iv) and, finally, the mass radicalism that exhibited itself in the electoral success of working-class parties in the immediate post-war years.

Thus an irreversible shift in the role of the state was countenanced in these years. A post-war political 'settlement' between representatives of capital and organised labour was essential to lay the basis for (what later transpired to be) the unprecedented boom of the next two decades. As part of this strategy, welfare reforms and the welfare state played an important role.

The emergence of the welfare state, as part of a post-war settlement between capital and labour and of a generally more interventionist state structure, was a general phenomenon of this period, but was perhaps most marked in Britain. This is not the place to investigate the differential effects of wartime experience on combatant nations,[32] but some unique features of the British experience should be mentioned. The British people experienced the collective mobilisation and widespread sacrifices, including aerial bombardment, of modern total war, but did not experience either occupation or defeat, yet suffered the relative weakening of their economy along with all European countries. In the political field the experience of wartime coalition government moderated the radical impact which the landslide Labour victory might have had. In the industrial field the growth of union membership during the war was combined with the establishment under Bevin of 'tripartism' as a means of controlling industrial conflict and securing strategic agreements between business and trade unions. This unique configuration of circumstances contributed to the key role which the welfare state (the very term originated in this period) played in post-war Britain. But underlying these specific national features were the twin forces distinguished above. The experience of modern total war *both* strengthened the leverage of the labour movement *and* gave further impetus to the centralisation of the state (partly in reaction to the first). The result was a rash of social legislation and the foundations of the welfare state in its present form.

The world leadership of the United States and the novel, more extended role of the state, formed the twin bases for the unprecedented boom within the capitalist world of the 1950s and 1960s. It is not my intention to discuss the reasons for the post-war boom in this book but, since it forms the indispensable backcloth to the period which saw the rise of the modern welfare state, a few words on the topic are merited. Under US leadership a set of international institutions were developed which provided a viable (for a time) framework within which international trade and specialisation could develop: the IMF, GATT, the OECD, NATO, the UN. The importance of this international framework in avoiding a repetition of the inter-war slide to protectionism and stagnation was immense.

The second basis for post-war expansion was the increased role of the state, resulting from wartime experience, the ever-increasing 'socialisation of production', and the new international balance of forces. In some countries, such as Britain, this took the form of an explicit commitment to pursue full-employment policies by means of Keynesian economic techniques. Elsewhere, such as France, there was an emphasis on positive economic planning by the state. In all countries, state intervention in the economy escalated. So the growth of welfare policies during this period must be situated within the context of a general extension in the role of the state.

The post-war boom, established on these foundations, gained a rapid momentum of its own. The 'catching-up' process explains a great deal of the dynamism of countries like Germany and Japan, which could utilise the advanced, war-stimulated technology of the United States to achieve extremely high growth rates. By contrast, economic growth in America itself was limited to that permitted by new technological innovations.[33] This uneven development within the advanced capitalist world stimulated an unprecedented development in the internationalisation of the capitalist system. The rapid growth of world trade, the spread of the multinational corporation and the development of international credit based initially on the dollar, resulted in a close interdependence of the capitalist nations on one another. The world boom generated further developments in its wake, such as the mobilisation of large supplies of labour, either from older, declining sectors of economies (in particular agriculture) or from housewives, or the vast migration of labour such as that from the peripheral countries of southern Europe. (The structural shift in the labour force was a corollary or consequence of the post-war boom not, however, its cause.)

Nevertheless this, plus the rapid growth of labour productivity, failed to prevent the major supplies of labour being absorbed and, therefore, 'over-full employment' from developing. This in turn has strengthened the bargaining power of labour in all post-war countries, though at different tempos in each. Thus, whether or not there was an initial commitment to pursue full-employment policies, the very dynamism of the capitalist economies brought it about by the end of the 1950s at the latest. This in turn increased the economic and political leverage of the organised working class to obtain improvements not only in money wages but also in the 'social wage'. It also contributed to a series of novel politico-economic problems, of which endemic inflation was the most important and pervasive (see Chapter 7). In turn this engendered a further series of state initiatives and a restructuring of the state in order to implement them. The variety of state interventions by the 1960s was very wide, ranging from the 'corporatist' policies of Britain and Sweden, through 'etatist' centralised initiatives in France and Italy to managed free-enterprise capitalism in Germany and the United States.[34] But in all of them a further centralisation of the state structure was visible. This augmented the direct pressure from the labour movement for, among other things, new forms of social policies in the fields of education, income maintenance, health and housing. Thus a second period of welfare expansion took place: for all OECD countries combined, average expenditure on education, income maintenance and housing rose from 13 per cent of GDP in the early 1960s to 18 per cent of GDP in the early 1970s.[35]

In some ways the British experience at this time reveals this scenario in heightened form; in other ways it is unique. Two features have dominated the economic, social and political development of post-war Britain and provide the indispensable backcloth against which to situate the British welfare state: the defensive economic strength of the organised working class and labour movement, and the long-term weakness of the British economy. The reasons for the first[36] include the long period of uninterrupted trade-union growth since the early 1930s (*cf.* Germany), British unions' unification and cohesiveness (*cf.* France and other countries where unions have for long been divided along confessional lines), and the extent they are organised at the point of production via the shop-steward system (*cf.* Sweden). Among the major countries of the capitalist world, Britain has the highest union membership—about one half of the labour force, compared with Germany 38 per cent, the United States 22 per cent, France and Japan 20 per cent. To these strengths should be added the close links with the Labour Party.

The other outstanding feature is the long-term relative decline of the British economy, its slow rate of growth and its early slide into crisis. Hobsbawm convincingly argues that Britain's long-term decline since the late nineteenth century is a consequence of its early industrialisation. The Empire, the fruits of British capital's pioneering role, provided the cocoon into which it retreated and which in the end almost smothered it. The export of capital and the importance of the City and of banking capital eventually drained Britain of the necessary resources for competitive investment. In the post-war period, Purdy argues, it has been not so much the direct economic costs of the old imperial connection, but the political consequences which explain the continuing decline.[37] The lack of fusion between *banking* capital (the City of London) and *industrial* capital (the large corporations) and the dominance of the former within the British state until the early 1960s, meant that essential policies to secure its industrial regeneration, for example entry into the EEC and the devaluation of sterling, were only belatedly applied.[38] The turn-around in economic policies in the early 1960s[39] coincided with growing trade-union influence and the return to power of a labour government.

Once again this combination of circumstances had ramifying effects on social policy: the expansion of higher education, the break with the Beveridge tradition in social security, the reversal of previous housing policies, all reflected 'economic' as well as 'social' demands and, behind these, the interaction of the two sets of forces analysed in this chapter. One aspect of this was the further development of 'corporatist' or 'tripartite' structures and processes in Britain, discussed in more detail in Chapter 7.

Our purpose in this section has been to demonstrate how and why the growth of class pressure and the centralisation of the state generated the modern welfare state in the post-war capitalist world in general and in Britain in particular. As a result the era of the welfare state is synonymous with the era of advanced capitalism.

5
THE EXPANSION OF SOCIAL EXPENDITURE

The forces outlined above have generated a massive expansion in public expenditure on the social services, or state social expenditure. This chapter looks in turn at the nature and distribution of social expenditure, at the immediate causes of its growth and, finally, at some of the consequences for the finance, administration and planning of the welfare state. Much of this chapter focuses on the UK situation, but international comparisons are made where possible: they show that the major features here are paralleled in all other advanced capitalist countries.

We need some benchmark against which to measure changes in expenditure over time and to compare expenditures between countries. Since the war, price levels and money incomes have continually risen, and so have real income levels for most years. This means that absolute changes in expenditure, measured in money terms, can be misleading. When comparing spending levels across national boundaries we have the further problem of deciding on 'correct' exchange rates for different currencies. The benchmark that is most commonly used is gross domestic product (GDP) or gross national product (GNP).

The value added (that is the value of output minus value of inputs) in the production of all goods and services in a country during a year is its GDP. In the process of producing these goods and services in a capitalist economy, incomes are received—wages for workers, profits for capital owners, rent for landowners. These incomes result from the expenditure of those who pay for the final goods and services produced. The money values of these three magnitudes are by definition equal—they provide three different ways of measuring GDP:

Value of net domestic *output* ≡ value of domestically generated *income* ≡ value of *expenditure* on domestic output of final goods and services.

GNP is simply GDP with property income earned by UK residents (individuals and corporations) added in and that paid abroad to foreign residents subtracted out. However, the difference nowadays is relatively small for most advanced countries: in the United Kingdom in 1975 GDP was £93,146m, GNP was £94,095m.[1]

THE COST OF THE WELFARE STATE

The cost of the social services in Britain as a share of GNP has risen dramatically from around 4 per cent before the First World War to 29 per cent in 1975 (see Table 5.1). They now account for one half of all state expenditure. This growth has occurred discontinuously in three major stages, centred around the two world wars, the most recent period being the early 1960s onwards. During the First World War, the share of social spending in GNP more than doubled but then remained relatively stable at 10–12 per cent throughout the inter-war period. The Second World War saw state intervention climb to an all-time high, but with the coming of peace (and the Cold War), total state spending settled down at a much higher plateau of around 45 per cent of GNP. Within this total, social expenditure rose somewhat but not dramatically, and then levelled out again during the 1950s. In the early 1960s a third period of very rapid growth was inaugurated, both in the overall role of the state and, within it, of the welfare state. Social expenditure has grown from 18 to 29 per cent of GNP since 1961 and now amounts to one half of all state spending.

All the major social services have shared in this growth, but in different ways and degrees. Housing expenditure tended to rise following both world wars, but then to fall off (until the substantial increase in the 1970s). Social security fluctuated in the inter-war period, partly reflecting the unprecedented numbers unemployed, and surprisingly did not increase at all in the 1940s at the time when the Beveridge system was being enacted. It has grown subsequently however and remains the most costly portion of the welfare state. Health spending really increased with the foundation of the National

TABLE 5.1 *The growth of social expenditure in the UK*

| | *Percentage of GNP at factor cost* | | | | | | | |
	1910	*1921*	*1931*	*1937*	*1951*	*1961*	*1971*	*1975*
All social services	4.2	10.1	12.7	10.9	16.1	17.6	23.8	28.8
Social security	{	4.7	6.7	5.2	5.3	6.7	8.9	9.5
Welfare	{	1.1	1.8	1.8		{0.3	0.7	1.1
Health		2.2	2.8	2.6	4.5	4.1	5.1	6.0
Education		2.1	1.3	1.4	3.2	4.2	6.5	7.6
Housing	0.7	0.6	1.0	1.0	3.1	2.3	2.6	4.6
Infrastructure	1.8	4.5	3.2	2.8	3.6	4.8	6.3	6.8
Industry					6.9	4.9	6.5	8.3
Justice and law	0.6	0.8	0.8	0.7	0.6	0.8	1.3	1.5
Military	3.5	5.6	2.8	5.0	10.8	7.6	6.6	6.2
Debt interest and other	1.9	7.7	8.2	5.2	6.9	6.3	5.9	6.3
Total state expenditure	12.7	29.4	28.8	25.7	44.9	42.1	50.3	57.9
Total state revenue	11.0	24.4	25.0	23.8	42.7	38.5	48.6	46.6
Borrowing requirement	1.7	5.0	3.8	1.9	2.2	3.6	1.7	11.3

NOTES For more precise definitions of each term see Table 2 of I. Gough, 'State expenditure in advanced capitalism', *New Left Review* 92 (1975) p. 60.
SOURCES A. Peacock and D. Wiseman, *The Growth of Public Expenditure in the UK*, 2nd edn (Allen and Unwin, 1966); CSO, *Social Trends* (HMSO).

Health Service: in effect, a transfer took place from private to public spending in 1948. Thereafter, however, its cost *fell* as a share of GNP until the 1960s. Since that time expenditure on the health service and on the mushrooming personal social services has accelerated. Lastly, expenditure on education displays the most consistent growth throughout this century, but again it has accelerated dramatically during the last fifteen years or so with the expansion of higher education. Table 5.1 also shows that many other items of state expenditure have risen, the major exception being military spending which has fallen in the post-war period since the Korean War peak (though it is still high by historical standards).

Turning to the other major countries in the OECD we observe the pattern noted in Chapter 4: different patterns and structures of expenditure between countries, but similar trends in all of them (see Table 5.2). The size and pattern of spending on the three major social services in the United Kingdom is remarkably similar to the average for all OECD countries.[2] Japan is in a class of its own (among the major economies shown in the table), spending only 10 per cent of its GDP on those social services. The US government spends relatively more on education and much less on health, though total spending on health (including private health outlays) is higher than in any other country. The EEC countries spend relatively more on all items, especially on income maintenance, averaging around 21 per cent of GDP. The highest proportion are found in Sweden, Denmark (22 per cent) and the Netherlands (27 per cent of GDP).

However, all the advanced capitalist countries exhibited the same trends in the later post-war period as did the United Kingdom: public expenditure rising as a share of GDP, and social expenditure rising as a share of public expenditure. Table 5.2 shows the ratio of growth rates for each item to that of GDP: for the OECD as a whole, public health spending expanded 75 per cent faster than GDP in the 1960s, income maintenance 42 per cent faster and education 38 per cent faster. In every country the social services increased their claims on GDP in the 1960s and early 1970s.

So far we have considered state expenditure as a uniform mass without discriminating between its different economic categories. But the resource impact of this total depends crucially on whether the state is using up resources which would otherwise be available for other purposes, or is merely transferring spending power from one group to another. This important distinction between *resource*

TABLE 5.2 *Social expenditure in the early 1970s: major OECD countries*

Country	Income maintenance		Health		Education		Total
	% GDP in early 1970s	Elasticity early 1960s–early 1970s	% GDP in early 1970s	Elasticity* early 1960s–early 1970s	% GDP in early 1970s	Elasticity early 1960s–early 1970s	% GDP in early 1970s
UK	7.7	1.68	4.9	1.42	5.6	1.27	18.2
USA	8.0	1.64	3.1	2.54	6.0	1.30	17.1
Japan	2.8	1.42	3.5	1.86	3.6	0.99	9.9
EEC	10.6	1.45	–	–	5.1	1.39	–
France	12.4	1.09	5.5	1.72	4.5	1.02	22.4
Germany	12.4	1.09	5.5	2.09	4.2	1.23	22.1
Italy	10.4	1.63	5.3	1.78	4.0	1.31	19.7
Canada	7.3	1.64	5.4	2.03	7.7	1.68	20.4
Sweden	9.3	1.93	7.3	1.85	7.1	1.41	23.7
OECD†	8.7	1.42	4.8	1.75	4.6	1.38	18.1

NOTES *Elasticity* = ratio of growth rates to growth of GDP between early 1960s and early 1970s.
* Elasticity of current expenditure on health only; all other figures refer to current plus capital expenditure.
† Geometric mean of all OECD countries.
SOURCE OECD, *Public Expenditure on Income Maintenance Programmes* (July 1976), *Public Expenditure on Health* (July 1976), *Public Expenditure on Education* (July 1976).

expenditure and *transfers* will recur throughout the rest of this book, so we shall spend a little time on it here.

Almost all the spending on health, education and personal social services is resource expenditure; that is it consumes labour, energy, buildings and other real inputs. So too does capital expenditure on new local-authority housing. On the other hand, pensions, for example, are a transfer item. The social-security system dispenses money to various groups: the elderly, families with children, the sick, the unemployed and so forth. But it is the pensioner etc. who spends the money and thus lays claim to real resources: food, housing, clothing, fuel, cigarettes and so on. The government merely transfers purchasing power.

If we now return to our definition of GDP, we find this breaks down into the following major categories of final expenditure:

GDP = Consumption spending (C) + Government resource
spending (G_r) + Investment expenditure (I)
+ Exports (X) − Imports (M)

Note here that only government resource spending is included because only this produces an output of goods and services. Government transfers (G_t) will finally appear under consumer spending (C), or under investment (I) if they include capital grants to firms. It follows that to calculate $G_r + G_t$ as a proportion of GNP, as was done in Table 5.1, is a questionable procedure. We are not comparing like with like. It would be conceivable for total state spending to approach 100 per cent of the GNP and yet for the private capitalist economy to survive! But to say this is to reveal the sense behind that approach. For however the money is spent, the state must finance it in some way, so our omnibus measure of state expenditure does provide a meaningful index of the total impact of the state in the economy, so to speak.

Table 5.3 divides up state expenditure (still speaking of it as a whole at this point) in this crucial way for the same series of years as in Table 5.1. It shows that G_r and G_t have each accounted for roughly one half of total state expenditure (G) since the First World War. Resource expenditure was higher immediately after the Second World War, but since then transfers, especially social-security benefits, have risen rapidly to reduce this imbalance. So in terms of its claims on resources the state has grown slower this century, from

TABLE 5.3 *The resource impact of central and local government expenditure in the UK*

	Percentage of GNP							
	1910	1921	1931	1937	1951	1961	1971	1975
Resource spending	10.1	16.2	14.2	16.0	25.1	22.5	26.8	29.6
Transfer spending	2.6	13.2	14.6	10.0	19.8	19.6	23.5	28.3
Total state expenditure	12.7	29.4	28.8	25.9	44.9	42.1	50.3	57.9

SOURCES A. Peacock and D. Wiseman, *The Growth of Public Expenditure in the UK*, 2nd edn., (Allen and Unwin, 1966); CSO, *Social Trends* (HMSO).

10 per cent of GNP in 1910 to 30 per cent in 1975. Since the war it can be seen that the share of real spending has risen very little at all: it fell as a proportion of GNP in the 1950s but recovered in the 1960s and surged ahead in the 1970s. This slow growth is due to the constant fall in the share of military spending over this period from the Second World War and Korean War levels, which has released resources for other state services. Even so, real spending on the NHS and on housing also fell in the 1950s. The important conclusion is that, in 1975 British public expenditure totalled 58 per cent of GNP, but it pre-empted about 30 per cent of GNP (35 per cent if the nationalised industries are included).

From the point of view of its economic impact and the role of state spending on economic crises there is one further important distinction to be drawn. Government resource spending (G_r) consists of two quite separate items: (i) the wages and salaries of government employees, and (ii) purchases of equipment, buildings and other supplies from the private capitalist sector. Let us call these respectively G_w and G_p. Figure 5.1 illustrates the breakdown of total G thus arrived at:

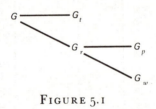

FIGURE 5.1

This last distinction can be illustrated by reference to the health service: part of its cost consists of the wages and salaries of doctors, nurses, technicians, porters, orderlies etc., and part the costs of drugs, equipment, electricity, new buildings and so forth.

It is public-sector employment that has expanded most noticeably, especially in the last decade or so (Table 5.4). Whilst the total labour force increased by 6 per cent from 1958–74, the numbers employed in the public sector rose by 15 per cent, and virtually the entire increase was concentrated in the local authorities.

The social services accounted for much of this rise. In 1974 over two million were employed in education, health and local-authority social services. The major groups of social-service workers today are teachers (over 600,000), nurses (nearly 400,000), ancillary health and

TABLE 5.4   *The public-sector labour force*

	Numbers in 1974 (millions)	% increase 1959–74
Local authorities	2.8	+60
Central government civilian	1.7	+6
Total government civilian	4.6	+34
Public corporations	1.9	−2
Total public sector (including HM forces)	6.8	+15
Private sector	18.3	+3
Total labour force	25.1	+6

SOURCE   R. Klein *et al.*, *Constraints and Choices* (Centre for Studies in Social Policy, 1976) Table 13.

hospital staff (about 250,000), school-meals staff and other ancillary education workers (about 500,000) and local-authority workers in the personal social services (about 200,000). Because much of the extra labour force was relatively unskilled, much of it part-time, and because earnings in the public sector lagged somewhat between 1959–74, the total wage bill rose proportionately slower than the numbers employed.[3] Nevertheless the weight of wages and salaries in total social-service costs has increased in Britain since the war, and it is likely that this experience was repeated in other capitalist countries.

What then is the composition of government social-services spending at the present time? Table 5.5 provides a breakdown between our three categories. Education, health and welfare are the major employers in the welfare state and account for almost all wage costs. Health, housing and education, in that order, constitute the leading purchasers of private-sector output, which totals slightly less than wage costs. The third column shows that besides the social-security system, housing subsidies and education are also important elements of transfer expenditure. Overall, almost three-fifths of state welfare expenditure is resource spending on goods and services, and over one half of this (one-third of the total) comprises wage and salary costs. Each service obviously has a different make-up. Perhaps

TABLE 5.5   *The economic nature of social expenditure in 1975 (£ million)*

	Wages	Purchases	Transfers	Total
Social security	240	251	8427	8918
Education	4108	1505	1013	6626
NHS	2816	2356	30	5202
Personal social services	609	377	4	990
School meals and welfare foods	311	79	—	390
Housing	16	2305	1970	4291
Total	8100	6873	11444	26417
(Percentage)	31	26	43	100

SOURCE   CSO, *National Income and Expenditure 1965–75*, Tables 9.2 and 10.2.

most interesting is the scale of purchases made by the NHS: after the military, it is the single most important source of government demand for the products of the private (and nationalised) sector of the economy. Housing too is important in this respect, and the intense debates over the nationalisation of the drug industry and over local-authority direct works departments (where the state itself supplies the inputs) can be better appreciated in the light of this evidence: but more of this later.

THE CAUSES OF GROWING SOCIAL EXPENDITURE

What are the immediate reasons for the remarkable increase in social expenditure here and abroad in recent years? To answer this question it is helpful to distinguish four separate factors and look at the impact of each. These are:

(*i*)   rising relative costs;
(*ii*) population changes;
(*iii*) new and improved services;
(*iv*) growing social needs.

We say 'immediate' reasons advisedly, for behind these factors, especially the third and fourth, lie the major determinants of social policy discussed in Chapter 4 above. But the analysis below helps evaluate the expenditure impact of these wider forces and also focuses on the importance of semi-automatic factors working to raise welfare costs in all advanced capitalist countries.

(i) Rising relative costs. There is a tendency, for the relative costs of the social services to rise faster than the average, so that a higher level of spending is required year by year just to maintain standards. Of course, inflation affects all prices and needs to be discounted when looking at expenditure levels, but this is something over and above the rise in the general price level and is referred to as the 'relative price effect'. It applies only to state-provided services (G_r), not to transfers, and is of great importance in explaining the rising cost of the welfare state.

Because the social services (like all services) are very labour-intensive, and because there is less possibility of raising productivity to offset higher wages, the relative costs of providing them rise year by year. Indeed, normal expectations are that the quality of service provided is higher when there are more doctors per patient, more social workers per client, more teachers per pupil and so on. This is in sharp contrast to industry where a rise in productivity means a fall in the labour time required to produce a car, or a ton of coal. Of course there is a big problem in measuring the output of the social services, independent of the numbers employed. In the absence of free market prices, which in a capitalist economy provide a simple undisputed yardstick, there is no way in which the 'value' of their output can be assessed. To use 'shadow prices' is to inscribe an alien capitalist logic upon a sector of the economy shielded from the operation of the law of value, or market pressures. The usual means is to assume that labour productivity in the social services is static and then to measure output in terms of the numbers employed.

On this basis the relative costs of the social services and most other state sectors have risen unremittingly here and abroad. For all OECD countries taken together, the average increase in the general price level from 1963 to 1973 was 4.5 per cent per annum, whereas that for government services (G_r) was 6.4 per cent—over one-third faster. In the social services, higher relative costs accounted for one half of the rise in spending on hospital services and education in the OECD over this period.[4] In Britain, higher relative costs were especially important in the early 1970s; from 1970/1 to 1974/5 they increased as follows:[5]

Housing: 41 per cent faster than the general price index
Health and personal social services: 13 per cent faster than the
general price index
Education: 7 per cent faster than the general price index
Social security: 1 per cent faster than the general price index

Though this is a general trend accounted for by the 'technology'
of these services, there are specific factors which affect its tempo.
On the wages side the strength of public-sector unions is important.
The rise in the relative costs of the health and personal social
services and of education in 1975 largely reflected the pay rises won
by nurses and teachers as a result of more militant struggle.[6] The
successful attempts by nurses to reduce their hours of work and by
teachers to relinquish supervision of school meals (so that an extra
army of part-time women are now employed to fulfil this function)
are further examples of the way that growing unionisation and
militancy in the public sector has raised the relative costs of the
social services. But behind this lies an important shift in the social-
service labour force. In the inter-war years they were to a much
greater extend staffed by single women working for very low pay.
Demographic and economic changes in the post-war era have
virtually dried up this traditional source of labour, requiring the
social services to compete in the broader labour market and offer
more attractive pay and conditions of work. For these and other
reasons then, the costs of wages (G_w) have recently (since 1974)
risen faster than normal in the state sector.

(ii) Population changes. Since the war the population of the United
Kingdom has increased by about six million. This alone would, of
course, generate higher needs for everything from maternity beds
to remand homes, if nothing else changed.

But more important in explaining rising costs *per capita* is the
change in the structure of the population, particularly the age
structure. The respective increases in the different age groups in the
United Kingdom this century has been as shown in Table 5.6.[7]

Within the same overall increase for each period there is a
dramatic change in the age structure. Whilst in the first period the
population of working age increased much faster than the total, in
the post-war period it hardly increased at all and the growth of the
'dependent' population (children plus elderly) was correspondingly

TABLE 5.6   *Population increases in the UK*

	1911–41(%)	*1941–69*(%)
Children (0–14)	−22	+31
Adults (15–59/64)	+24	+4
Elderly (60/65+)	+97	+54
All ages	+15	+15

large. This tremendous reversal in the age structure of the population predominantly reflects past changes in birth rates. In the inter-war period, the birth rate was falling, but the then working population was drawn from the 'cohort' born before the First World War when birth rates were higher, whilst the older generation was born at an earlier period still when birth rates were even higher. By the post-war period, the low inter-war cohort moved into the working-age groups, and this smaller number had to support rising numbers of elderly from the pre-First World War generation *and* rising numbers of children in the post-Second World War generation. Clearly the prospect for the last quarter of this century is for a more balanced age structure whatever the future course of birth and death rates. The number of dependents per 100 working people, having fallen from sixty-one in 1911 to forty-nine in 1941 and risen rapidly to sixty-six in 1969, will now begin to fall again. The population trends noted above have been paralleled in most advanced capitalist countries: for example, in every OECD country without exception the proportion of elderly people rose from 1955–69.

All this has a powerful impact on social expenditure since the major users of the welfare state are those in the dependent age groups, namely children and the elderly. As a result the post-war period has been characterised by increasing pressure on the major social services, combined with a lower growth in the working population to provide them. The pressure on costs in social work and the personal social services in the United Kingdom can be gauged from Table 5.7[8]

As a result, especially of the ageing of the population in the recent past, the government calculates that spending on the personal social services needs to grow at 2 per cent a year just to maintain standards. In the OECD as a whole, the ageing of the population has had a

TABLE 5.7   *Growth of expenditure on personal social services in the UK*

Age	Expenditure per head (£) on the personal social services	Rate of increase in age groups 1961–73(%)
0–15	15	+9
16–64	5	+1
65–74	20	+20
75+	95	+18
All age groups	15	+6

big impact on social-security programmes, accounting for one-third of the increase in their expenditure.

How much of the growth in British social expenditure is explained by these two 'automatic' factors? Figure 5.2 tries to answer this question for the period 1965–75 in three major sectors. Expenditure on the NHS, for example, increased by 314 per cent in money terms, but much of this reflected general inflation; taking account of this reduced its growth to 70 per cent. However, this still ignores the *relative* increase in NHS costs, so that the growth in real expenditure (in terms of what it will purchase) was only 40 per cent. Taking account of the ageing of the population and other demographic factors reduced the real increase per user to 27 per cent over the ten-year period. Our two factors considered above therefore account for almost three-quarters of the expenditure increase in education, over three-fifths in health and one-half in the rapidly growing personal services sector (ignoring general inflation here). But what of the remainder? Does all this represent a real improvement in standards?

(iii) New and improved services. This covers two distinct trends: first, an extension in the coverage of social services as more groups in the population and more categories of need become eligible for benefits. Often this takes the form of a shift from private to public responsibility for a particular area, as when Medicare and Medicaid were introduced in the United States. It includes the introduction of completely new services as well as the extension of existing ones to new groups and contingencies. All these reflect an *extensive* growth of the welfare state. Second, improvements in the level of service

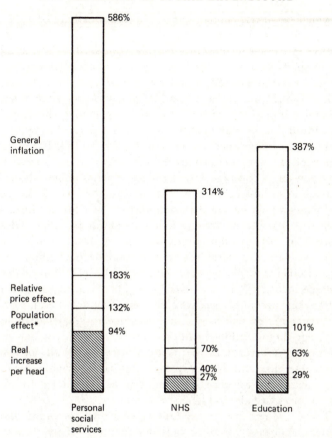

FIGURE 5.2 *Percentage increases in government expenditure on services 1965–75*[9]

* This assumes the following increases in 'need' stemming from population changes alone:

Education + 27 per cent, derived from a calculation of the increase in the 5–14 year old age-group,

NHS + 10 per cent, and

Personal social services + 20 per cent, using the figures in *The Government's Expenditure Plans* (1977), vol. II (HMSO), p. 80, for the second half of the 1970s.

SOURCE CSO, *National Income and Expenditure 1965–67*, Tables 2.1, 2.4 and 10.2 (HMSO).

provided per head. Among services in kind this may be measured by their utilisation rates, among cash benefits by the level of benefits relative to average incomes or some other standard. (These measures are of course equivocal—they assume that more necessarily means better.) These trends reflect an *intensive* growth of the welfare state.

The OECD has recently conducted a series of studies on the respective importance of these factors in explaining the growth of expenditure on income maintenance, health and education. They find that the importance of each differs (taking all OECD countries together from the early 1960s to the early 1970s). In *income maintenance*, the extension of coverage and eligibility explains almost all the real increase in social-security spending (that is, after taking account of the demographic impact discussed above). Benefits per head kept pace with the rise in average living standards but they did little more than this. In other words the cost of social security in the advanced capitalist world rose because more people became eligible for more benefits, not because the level of benefits rose relative to average incomes.[10] In the *health* field, both factors played a role. After taking account of relative costs (very important here), over half the remaining growth in spending was due to greater coverage of and eligibility for public health schemes, and slightly under half to the greater utilisation of the health services—especially of general medical services and drugs. On the other hand, virtually the entire real increase in *education* spending was accounted for by higher utilisation, especially in higher education.

These findings are for all OECD countries combined and, of course, hide great variations between countries. If we turn to the United Kingdom, we find that greater coverage (extensive welfare development) has been of little importance over the last three decades. The major social services were established in the 1940s—for example the present social security and national health system in 1948. This means that by comparison with many other countries the British welfare state was by this time more 'mature' and extensions to it since then have been relatively minor. The growth in real spending shown in Figure 5.1 therefore reflects rising benefit levels, higher rates of utilisation and/or new services. In practice, all three have occurred.

First, the level of most social-security benefits have increased faster than the general rate of inflation since 1948, and most have risen faster than average earnings, especially post-tax earnings (the major exceptions are family allowances since their inception, and short-term benefits and unemployment benefits since 1973).[11] In the personal social services, the trends towards smaller residential homes for the elderly, the mentally and physically handicapped and children undoubtedly represents an improvement over the barracks of Victorian times and have raised unit costs. Second, in common with other countries, utilisation of education and some health services has expanded. Sometimes different sectors of welfare services expand in tandem, as when more field social workers result in more children being brought into care. In the field of social security the uptake of many means-tested benefits has grown, partly as the result of deliberate emphasis on selective policies. Lastly, new legislation creates new services or lays fresh obligations on central and local government. For example, in the personal services, recent years have witnessed a plethora of legislation—the 1969 Children and Young Persons Act, the 1970 Chronically Sick and Disabled Persons Act, the 1971 White Paper on the Mentally Handicapped and the 1975 Children's Act—all of which increases social expenditure.[12]

Adding all these factors together it would seem undeniable that real improvements in certain sectors of the welfare state have occurred. According to the OECD:

> In most of the Common Market countries social security provisions in the fields of minimum old age pensions, survivor allowances, finance or direct provision of medical services, medical provisions and income maintenance for the disabled have been improved considerably in substance and coverage.[13]

But before we can be certain of this, we must consider our last factor—the growth of new social needs. If the *need* for services increases through time, the extension of services may not mark any improvement in the level of need-satisfactions.

(iv) Growing social needs. This raises some extremely difficult, but interesting, conceptual questions. At one level this process is easily understood. For example, the escalation of unemployment since 1967 and especially since the 1974 slump has automatically increased the 'need' for unemployment benefit. Between 1974 and 1975 alone the numbers in Britain receiving unemployment benefit and/or supplementary benefit for unemployment 'doubled and the costs

doubled too—from about £400 million to over £800 million. Clearly, to ignore the growth in need when seeking to explain this growth of expenditure would be absurd.

But at a much more general level the unplanned relentless drive of capitalist development continually generates new needs. Titmuss[14] has analysed one of the crucial functions of the welfare state as the compensation of victims for the *diswelfares* they suffer as a result of 'economic progress'. Numerous 'social problems', from the middle-aged redundant to the victims of urban redevelopment to the thalidomide children, can be interpreted as the social costs associated with rapid economic and technological progress. We have already had cause to reject a purely mechanistic explanation of the develop-ment of social policy along these lines, but as a tool in evaluating the impact of the social services it is extremely useful. For example, the redevelopment of cities predominantly results from the anony-mous workings of the property market, with local and central government doing little more than to modify, regulate or even encourage these powerful forces.[15] But consider the new social needs this has generated. Young families with children are more and more segregated from their parents who may previously have provided an essential support function. If the mother now wishes to work she must look to local-authority day-nurseries or some other substitute. If, as has happened, the government refuses to extend day-care provisions, a series of unsatisfactory alternatives will inevitably be generated, such as the spread of unregistered childminders.[16] On the other hand, housebound elderly people are also separated from their immediate family and require increasing state assistance via home-helps or residential care.[17] This is not of course to argue that such changes may not be desirable in themselves, but the net result is to raise the need for personal social services and hence of expenditure on them. If, on the contrary, state policy is to shift more responsibility on to the 'family and community' (as following the Seebohm re-organisation) and if in practice this reads simply 'the family', then the physical and psychological burdens on individuals will increase disproportionately.

We are now in a position to formulate the effects of increasing needs more rigorously.[18] It is essential to draw a sharp distinction between the outputs of welfare services and the final need-satisfactions enjoyed by their consumers. This requires that the latter can be measured independently of the former. It is not my intention to discuss the literature on measuring need-satisfactions here, but suffice it to note that indices of health, mobility, independence and other basic needs have been suggested and developed in recent years.[19] We are still a long way from being able to relate these to the inputs of social services provided but, at any rate, the distinction can be drawn in theory. If, then, capitalist development constantly generates new needs, it is conceivable that a continual growth in the output of welfare services may not result in a similar growth in the need-satisfactions of clients. These may even fall. In other words the social services may have to keep on running in order simply to stand still. The effects of the recent cuts in the welfare state are therefore much more critical than consideration of expenditure levels alone would suggest.

The point argued above is illustrated in the lower half of Figure 5.3. Part or all of an increase in the output of services may be necessary to cope with new needs. For example, the numbers of children in day-nurseries rose from 22,000 in 1966 to 26,000 in 1974, and the numbers of elderly receiving home-help rose from 329,000 to 514,000.

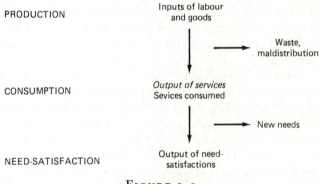

FIGURE 5.3

Yet the effects of more single-parent families and of increased isolation of the elderly may well alone have generated a faster increase in the need for these two services. We cannot say for certain, but on the available evidence it is highly likely. Again, services for the mentally ill have expanded in all advanced capitalist countries, but this must be set against the 'enormous rise in the prevalence of mental illnesses'.[20]

Figure 5.3 also shows a second source of 'loss' widening the gap between expenditure on producing services and final need-satisfactions still more: maldistribution or waste in the organisation or delivery of the services. The reorganisation of social-service departments in the 1970s, for example, is widely thought to have resulted in the spread of bureaucratisation, unneccessary clerical and supervisory work etc. If there is any truth in this accumulating evidence then again the growth of expenditure in this area over-estimates the real level of services provided. We return to these questions in the next two chapters. For the time being we should note that rising costs, changing population structure and the emergence of new needs probably account for almost all of the growth in social expenditure since the Second World War. Very little, or conceivably none at all, represents a real improvement in the satisfaction of needs.

FINANCE, ADMINISTRATION AND PLANNING: THE CENTRALISATION OF THE WELFARE STATE

What are the consequences of the growth of the welfare state and social expenditure in the post-war era? We shall look here at just three areas: the finance of welfare spending, the role of local government in its provision, and central government administration and planning.

Whatever the immediate reasons for the growing cost of the welfare state it has to be financed by one means or another. There are three basic ways of doing this—by raising taxes, by charging for state services and by borrowing. *Taxation* has always provided the bulk of government finance in all OECD countries. It includes not only the direct taxation of the incomes of households and firms, but also indirect taxes, customs and excise duties, social-security contributions, local rates and property taxes and various capital and wealth taxes. *Trading income* comprises the revenue obtained from those government services which are sold (whether at a market or subsidised price), such as council-house rents in Britain, together with miscellaneous charges made for certain services, such as NHS prescription charges. *Government borrowing* must inevitably make up the remainder of expenditure not covered by these two sources of revenue.

Now the dramatic increase in state expenditure of all sorts was not financed by means of a long-term growth in the state borrowing requirement until the mid-1970s. Table 5.1 shows that state revenue has risen roughly in line with expenditure in the United Kingdom this century (with a brief exception after the First World War), from 11 per cent of GNP in 1910 to almost one-half of GNP in 1971. Of this the vast bulk is from taxation—before the war, trading income was insignificant and since then it has amounted to 6–7 per cent of GNP. This pattern was repeated in all OECD countries in the post-war period with the crucial exception of the United States. Excluding the United States total taxation in all other OECD countries rose by 4.7 per cent per annum from the mid-1950s to the late 1960s: *faster* than the growth of all current expenditure which averaged 4.4 per cent per annum. (In the United States a large government deficit appeared in the 1960s as a result of the state's inability or unwillingness to finance the war in south-east Asia by raising taxes.) But in the unprecedented depression of the mid-1970s, government borrowing has risen to record levels in many countries. In the United Kingdom between 1971 and 1975 the gap between expenditure and revenue widened to 11 per cent of GNP, requiring state borrowing to the tune of £11 billion in 1975. The causes and consequences of this 'fiscal crisis of the state' are discussed in the next chapter. For the moment we should note that the growth of the state's welfare and other activities within advanced capitalism has also occasioned a vast increase in taxation.

The make-up of this enormous volume of taxation in the United Kingdom in 1975 was:

Direct taxes	Income taxation	43%	61%
	Social-security contributions	18%	
Indirect taxes	Expenditure taxes	27%	
	Local rates	10%	
Taxes on capital		2%	
Total (= 100%)		£37.9 billion	
Direct taxes—on employees		45%	61%
—on companies		16%	

Three-fifths of the total comes from direct taxation including social-security contributions (which are a compulsory deduction from income like any other tax). Of this amount, the major share (three-quarters and still rising) is levied from individual workers via income tax and national insurance contributions. Expenditure taxes, chiefly the duties on tobacco, alcohol and petrol, plus VAT, account for just over one-quarter and local-authority rates (a tax on property) a further 10 per cent, whilst the taxation of capital is virtually insignificant. Over time it is direct taxation that has expanded most rapidly to finance the increasing role of the state—before the First World War it accounted for less than one-third of the total—and within this rising total an increasing share has been shifted away from companies on to employees. Until the 1970s the yield of indirect taxation oscillated around one-third of the total, but it has recently fallen fast. Local rates have gradually declined as a significant source of revenue, from over 30 per cent before the First World War to 10 per cent today: a trend whose repercussions for the finance and future of local government is discussed below.[21]

Most of these trends are evident throughout the advanced capitalist world:[22] the growth in personal income taxes and social-security taxes, the stagnation of expenditure taxes, the decline to very low levels of corporate taxation, and the shift away from local to central taxation. But just as with patterns of state expenditure, the similarity of *trends* masks very different *structures* of taxation. As a proportion of GDP in 1973–5 the total tax burden varied from 47 per cent in Norway to 21 per cent in Japan. The Scandinavian countries and the Netherlands occupied the top of the table, the EEC countries an intermediate position (the UK share was 35 per cent) and the United States (29 per cent) near the bottom. The Continental European countries place greater reliance on social-security contributions than the rest of the world, whereas in the United States and Japan expenditure taxes are lower and company taxes higher than elsewhere. On the other hand there is some evidence of 'harmonisation' between British and European tax and social-security patterns in recent years.

The respective roles of central and local government in getting and spending this money is also of great importance. The bulk of spending on education, housing and the personal social services is undertaken by local authorities in the United Kingdom. In other countries, such as the United States, local government still plays a role in the administration of income-maintenance programmes. Local government is clearly a part of the state apparatus in capitalist societies, but it matters a great deal for political, economic and social reasons that it still plays an important role in the provision of social services. In 1975, education, housing and the personal social services accounted for two-thirds of all local-authority spending in the United Kingdom. If we take all local-authority expenditure, it has grown rapidly as a share of GNP, particularly since the early 1960s:

1951	1961	1971	1973	1975
9.8%	11.4%	15.5%	17.1%	18.6%

As a share of combined central and local spending it has also risen: from one-quarter in 1951 to about one-third in the 1970s. Moreover, over three-quarters of local expenditure is on goods and services, so its resource impact is proportionately greater than central government—as the mushrooming number of local-authority workers indicates (Table 5.4).

Clearly, local authorities are major agencies for spending money on the social services. At the same time, we have seen that they are not a major source of government finance: local rates raise less than one-tenth of government revenue. Rates are an inherently static tax: their revenue yield does not rise automatically year by year as does that of income tax. Each year a higher rate poundage must be deliberately levied by the local authority, and this is often a politically sensitive and unpopular decision. For this and other reasons, rates have met a smaller and smaller proportion of local-authority expenditure over the past ten years, falling from 39 per cent in 1965 to 27 per cent in 1975. At the same time, central government has re-established its position as an important source of loan finance for local capital projects.

We are then faced with an apparent paradox: local-authority spending, particularly on social services, has risen rapidly to one-third of total government expenditure, but local-authority rate income has fallen equally rapidly to one-tenth of government revenue. The gap has been filled by an increased flow of funds from central to local government, rising from 39 per cent in 1965 to 55 per cent in 1975—twice the yield from rates. In a nutshell, Whitehall raises more than it spends, and the town halls spend more than they raise. The principal mechanism for effecting the necessary transfer of funds is the system of central government grants—an increasingly important weapon of economic and social policy in its own right.

Like many other features of the British welfare state, the modern system of grants was established in 1948. Today the bulk is provided by the Rate Support Grant (RSG), but there are also certain specific grants, notably for the police forces and recent community programmes such as urban aid. The RSG is negotiated annually between central government and the local-authority associations. The former fixes the overall amount taking into account the desired level of local expenditure in the coming financial year and the share of this it considers should be raised by rates. The RSG total is then divided into three different 'elements'. The *needs* element accounts for the bulk, about two-thirds, and is related to the amount different areas need to spend on their major services, arising from such factors as the number of children of school age and the numbers of elderly. The *resources* element partially compensates for differences in authorities' rateable value per head and hence in their tax-raising capacity. This stems from the Exchequer Equalisation Grant of 1948 and is an important means of geographically redistributing resources, but it accounts for less than one-quarter of the RSG. The *domestic* element has been used in the 1970s to limit the increase in rates paid by householders, mainly as a component part of anti-inflation strategy. It is not possible here to examine the important influence of this grant structure on authorities of different types, such as the cities versus the counties. Though it is more centralised and thus more redistributive than, for example, the system in the United States, it is likely that the weight of the 'needs' element in the total offsets that of the 'resources' element and benefits those authorities with, for instance, a higher proportion of pupils staying on at school after sixteen (that is, more middle-class, affluent areas).[23] The relevant conclusion for our purposes, however, is that local authorities have become heavily dependent on central government for their finance.

The growing dependence of local authorities on Whitehall for current finance has recently exacerbated the already weak position of local government in England and Wales. 'Local government in modern England is the creation of Parliament . . . local authorities are obliged to provide certain services and allowed to provide others. They can do nothing else which costs money.'[24] Following the major recasting of local government in 1882, 1888 and 1894, the new authorities assumed major responsibility for the emerging social services. In some ways the inter-war period signalled their heyday, for since that time there has occured an apparently irreversible decline in their functions and financial autonomy (at the same time that their spending role has expanded). In 1934, responsibility for unemployment assistance was removed, in 1948 all public assistance and most health services, in 1974 their remaining health services plus water and sewage. Local government has also been re-organised in various ways. In 1974, local-authority areas were amalgamated to form fewer and larger areas. Within these larger authorities, corporate management practices have become more widespread.[25] The significant omission from this list of 'reforms' of local government is any restructuring of its financial basis, which has contributed to its growing dependence on central government.

Related to these two trends—the growing burden of taxation and the decline of local government—is a third: the restructuring of central government and its administration and planning of the social services. One index of this is the development of systematic procedures for the forward planning of public expenditure. Since 1961, rolling plans of public expenditure have been undertaken for each of the succeeding five years. Since 1969 these have been published as annual White Papers on Public Expenditure. Ultimately the major decisions on the level of public spending and the divisions between the departments will be taken in Cabinet, but the Chancellor of the Exchequer backed by the Treasury has a powerful voice in it. Glennerster[26] concluded that Britain with its strong executive branch, notably the Treasury, and relatively weak legislature has developed a powerful system of forward planning, in contrast to the United States. This is revealed in a recent development: the institution of *cash limits*. Two-thirds of voted expenditure is now subject to cash limits: a planned ceiling in cash terms on the extent to which initial estimates can be raised by supplementary votes. Through loan sanctions for capital spending and the RSG, Whitehall can also subject all local-authority spending to rigid cash limits. This machinery has played an important part in implementing the 'cuts' in public spending discussed in Chapter 7 below.

Another aspect of the restructuring of the machinery of central government has been the creation of large 'super-departments', such as the Department of Health and Social Security, operating with more managerial systems of control. Systematic forward planning of health and social-security services has been developed within this framework since 1974, the time when the structure of the NHS was altered to secure more effective central control. Glennerster concluded his survey of social-services budgeting in the United Kingdom and United States: 'What we see emerging for the National Health Service is the most managerial and the most hierarchical of planning systems we have encountered either in America or the United Kingdom.'[27]

The shift to central finance, the atrophy of local government and the spread of centralised planning systems within central government are all components of a process which I shall call the 'centralisation' of the welfare state. Though this has been argued with reference to developments within the United Kingdom, it is a trend with parallels throughout the advanced capitalist world. For example, in the United States the Federal Government has *financed* and *spent* a growing share of welfare expenditure, whereas the role of state and local governments has declined. State and local revenues are on the whole static but their expenditure, on the social services in particular, is very dynamic, whilst Federal tax revenues are highly dynamic, but its expenditure less so. Centralised budgetary control has also been extended in the United States this century, notably in 1920 when the Bureau of the Budget was formed, and in the early 1960s with the introduction of program-performance-budgeting systems (PPBS).[28] However, a comparison between the United Kingdom and the United States here reveals very interesting differences. Broadly speaking the British state, and the British welfare state, is much more centralised in terms of programmes, finance, administration and planning. In many respects the introduction of programme budgeting in the United States was a substitute for the lack of administrative reform and centralisation within the US state.[29] Britain, with its tightly circumscribed local government system, relatively weak legislature, long-established civil service and powerful Treasury, is much further along the road towards a centralised welfare state than is the United States. But both countries are travelling in the same direction.

This brings us back to the discussion in the previous chapter. The centralisation of the welfare state is not solely a response to the public expenditure implications of its growth, important as these are. It also reflects the political requirement for a 'class-conscious political directorate' able to represent the long-term interests of capital in the welfare field in the context of growing pressures for improved services from the labour movement and elsewhere in society. The relative strength of the British labour movement and the relative 'maturity' of the British welfare state provide further explanations of why this trend has developed to a much greater extent here.[30]

Nevertheless, economic pressures have come increasingly to the fore in accelerating this process in Britain, particularly since the early 1960s. The rapid growth of social expenditure here and abroad since that time has created novel problems and contradictions with which each nation state has had to grapple. The next chapter examines these problems in more detail.

6

THE WELFARE STATE AND
THE CAPITALIST ECONOMY

UNPRODUCTIVE LABOUR AND THE STATE

Has this extensive growth of state expenditure on the social services
and other items benefited or harmed the capitalist sector of the
economy? Has it promoted or fettered profitability and the accumulation of capital? This is the primary question which this chapter
seeks to answer. In doing so it will present the main features of
advanced capitalist economics in the form of simplified, abstract
models. These are used to help answer the question in the clearest
possible fashion, by ignoring numerous other factors which intrude
in the real world. In Chapter 7 we return to the 'here and now'
to consider in more detail the links between the growth of the
welfare state and the current economic crisis in Britain and elsewhere.

Since the 1940s, when the ideas of Keynes gained hold in
government circles, the orthodox answer to this question has focused
on the effect of state spending on aggregate *demand* in the economy.
State expenditure of any kind will raise the demand for goods and
services in the capitalist sector, though the manner in which this
occurs will depend on the category of expenditure (see Chapter 5,
pp. 8off.). In the case of state *purchases,* whether of drugs or arms,
it augments demand directly; in the case of *transfers* or state
employment it does so indirectly, by providing pensioners or state
employees with money to spend on consumer goods and services.
Thus, if nothing else in the economy changes, a rise in government
spending will increase aggregate demand in the economy, and if
there is unemployment and idle capacity at the time, output will
increase and unemployment will fall. This will occur directly if
public employment is increased, but it will happen just the same,
though not necessarily to the same extent, if transfers or purchases
are raised. Of course, other things will not necessarily remain the

same, and one of these is the level of taxation. We saw in Chapter 5 how the bulk of the growth in spending has been financed by a growth in taxation. Higher taxes reduce aggregate demand in the economy, either directly in the case of income tax and such like, or indirectly if expenditure taxes are raised (again provided that everything else remains the same—*ceteris paribus*).

It might be thought therefore than an equal increase in government spending and taxation would have a neutral impact on the level of demand and economic activity: higher taxation would subtract as much as the higher state spending would add. In fact, the exact balance will depend on the pattern of expenditure and taxation and other things: in the United Kingdom it has been estimated that tax revenue needs to exceed expenditure by about 8 per cent for the budget to have a neutral impact on national income.[1] Nevertheless the general principle holds: by adjusting tax levels appropriately the government can finance a growing level of state expenditure without affecting the level of aggregate demand and output. If the economy is underemployed an expansive budget can secure full employment; if the economy is already working at or near the full employment level, then this can be maintained, but a new problem arises: that of inflation. If agregate demand exceeds the supply of goods and services, then price rises will occur and spark off an inflationary spiral. Nevertheless, the basic propositions above are not affected. In terms of aggregate demand the growth of the welfare state is neither harmful nor beneficial so long as taxation is increased over time accordingly.

Now this all focuses on what political economy calls the *realisation* process. It explains how the state permits the output produced in the economy to be *realised*, or sold. It does not consider the effect of state activity on the *production* of this output in the first place. In Marxist terms it focuses on the realisation of surplus value and ignores its production.[2] But in recent years this, it has been appreciated, is a serious gap and other approaches have been developed in an attempt to fill it. Our aim in this section is to bring Marxist political economy to bear on these questions and, in particular, Marx's concepts of productive and unproductive labour.[3]

As we observed in Chapter 2, Marx demonstrated that the source of surplus value lay in the capitalist labour process. Here the worker exchanges his labour with capital to produce a value greater than the value of his labour power. Thus from the standpoint of capital that labour is productive which works for the self-expansion of capital by producing surplus value. All workers collectively engaged in production within the capitalist sector are productive on this basis. This leaves two distinct groups of workers who were thus categorised by Marx as *unproductive*. First, workers in the sphere of circulation, for example commercial workers, salesmen, advertising agents, many workers in the retail trade and so forth. Though they are employed by capital in just the same way as productive workers, they help *realise* the value embodied in commodities, they do not in any way *produce* it. This conception of unproductive labour has been criticised on several counts,[4] but we can safely leave it to one side in our present discussion.

The second group of unproductive workers is, however, of direct relevance to a study of the social services. It comprises those workers, notably in the state sector, who are not employed by capital at all, who therefore do not produce either value or surplus value. Workers in nationalised industries and other state trading enterprises are excluded from this category if they produce commodities for sale and in the process realise surplus value, or at least cover the costs of production. This leaves all state workers who produce services and goods that are not sold, hence do not assume the form of commodities: employees in the social services as well as the administrative, judicial and repressive apparatus of the state. All these groups of labour, Marx argued, are exchanged with revenue, not with capital. In these sectors money is not advanced to purchase labour power and means of production which are then put to work to produce a commodity which can be sold for a sum in excess of the original values embodied in its production. Instead, the outlays of labour and equipment are financed usually by taxation and the end product is simply 'consumed' directly as a use value: no surplus value is generated.

It should be noted here that Marx's concept of unproductive labour under capitalism has nothing whatsoever to do with whether the output produced is a good or a service, nor with its inherent usefulness or desirability. A capitalist firm may employ workers to produce services which realise surplus value for it in just the same way as the production of goods. Similarly, a useless or positively harmful product will embody productive labour if produced in the capitalist sector to realise a profit, whereas many social services meeting basic needs are unproductive if they do not realise profits and surplus value. No moral evaluations of any kind are implied in using the concepts of productive and unproductive labour.

What then is the purpose of the distinction? It is to explain the origin and extent of surplus value within capitalism and to understand the process of capital accumulation and growth. In a nutshell, the greater the surplus value generated by productive workers, the greater the potential rate at which capital can expand. It is a greater potential rate, because the surplus value can be utilised in ways other than purchasing more labour and equipment to produce yet more surplus value: it can be consumed by the capitalist, wasted in various ways or, crucial to our concern, it can be taxed by the state.

Now Marx nowhere deals directly with taxation in his writings, but there is no doubt that he saw the revenues to support state functionnaires in his time as originating in the surplus value produced by productive workers. Consequently, one school of Marxists regards all taxation and hence state expenditure as a drain on surplus value:

> In Marx's value analysis all taxes are taxes on capital and the source of all tax revenue is surplus value. Moreover, for Marx this is not merely some simplified abstract proposition, it is the normal state of affairs in reality. While taxes on labour may *temporarily* redistribute from labour to capital, the normal situation will be for a restoration of the (net) value of wages to the value of labour power.[5]

Thus wherever taxes are actually levied, they will ultimately, and fairly quickly, be passed on to capital and paid out of surplus value. It follows that any increase in state expenditure necessarily reduces the quantity of surplus value available for re-investment and this slows down the rate of capital accumulation and economic growth.

We have here a powerful argument concerning the contradictory impact of capitalist development. On the one hand, rising levels of state expenditure on the social services and other items are necessary to sustain the accumulation and reproduction of capital; on the other hand, the very growth of the state inhibits the accumulation of capital. I shall argue below that, whilst the mechanism adduced to explain this is faulty, the overall analysis is substantially correct. But first of all let us consider the arguments of two economists, Robert Bacon and Walter Eltis, whose analysis bears a superficial resemblance to that presented above. Their book, *Britain's Economic Problem: Too Few Producers*,[6] has had a wide impact and influenced government policy in Britain.

Bacon and Eltis argue that Britain has undergone a process of de-industrialisation since the early 1960s. There has taken place a far-reaching structural shift in employment over these years away from manufacturing industry and into the services, particularly the public services, and within this group particularly into the social services. From 1961–74 the numbers employed in manufacturing industry fell by 13 per cent, whilst public employment rose by one-third. Local government employees increased by 54 per cent, the numbers in education by 76 per cent and those in personal welfare services more than doubled. Though Bacon and Eltis recognise that there is a long-term shift in advanced capitalist economies from the manufacturing to the service sector, they argue that in those years the shift in Britain had no parallel in other countries. Their explanation of this fact is that the social services provide a cheap (that is, low-capital) means of maintaining full employment. The long-term causes of growing welfare services are not considered or recognised by them, so that the links with the development of advanced capitalism are missed. This results in a one-sided approach which ignores the growing necessity for state expenditure within these countries.

They divide the economy into two sectors—the *marketed* and *non-marketed* sectors—which closely resemble Marx's (second) distinction between productive and unproductive sectors.

The marketed sector comprises all those economic activities which produce goods or services for sale. The non-marketed sector produces goods and services which are not sold, such as 'defence, the National Health Service, most schools, policemen and civil servants'.[7] (Note that on this basis certain government activities fall within the marketed sector, such as the nationalised industries, the Post Office and council housing, so long as they yield enough revenue to cover costs. If they do not cover costs, then one could say that most of their output was marketed, whilst part 'would correspond to the non-marketed output of a civil service department'. On the other hand, certain private sector activities, for example the production of Concorde, fall almost entirely within the non-marketed sector, because they are massively subsidised from public funds.)

Now the incomes of 'unproductive workers' thus defined, for example social workers, can only be spent on the marketed products of the rest of the community. All exports are marketed, so these too must be provided in their entirety by the marketed sector. And, Bacon and Eltis argue, so must all investment goods. Consequently:

> The marketed output of industry and services taken together must supply the total private consumption, investment and export needs of the whole nation.
>
> A difficulty Britain has suffered from since 1961 is that the proportion of the nation's labour force that has been producing marketed output has been falling year by year; at the same time those who have had to rely on others to produce marketed output for them, civil servants, social workers, and most teachers and medical workers, have become increasingly numerous, and they have had to satisfy their requirements by consuming goods and services that diminishing numbers of market sector workers are producing.[8]

In other words, the growth of unproductive state employment has simultaneously reduced the share of marketed output *and* increased the claims on it. As a result they estimate that government claims on the output of the marketed sector soared from $41\frac{1}{2}$ per cent in 1961 to $60\frac{1}{2}$ per cent in 1974: an increase of 19 per cent. Consequently, '19 per cent less remained for those who actually produced the economy's entire marketed output'. They recognise that state spending other than on 'unproductive workers', for example on pensions, purchases from the private sector, subsidies, investment grants etc., etc., will also increase *claims* on marketed output (the numerator), but they will not of themselves reduce the *size* of the marketed sector (the denominator). The growth of state employment on the other hand both increases the numerator *and* reduces the denominator. (Those readers interested in a further analysis of these issues should turn to Appendix D, where a numerical example is also provided.)

So far the analysis has been conducted in terms of two sectors of the economy, with no distinction drawn between capital and labour, profits and wages, within the marketed (what we have called the capitalist) sector. The growth of all state spending implies a growing tax burden on this sector, and Bacon and Eltis seek to prove that this was borne by profits in Britain in the 1960s and early 1970s. The consequent fall in post-tax profits resulted in a rapid fall in the share of national output going into investment in the marketed sector and, as a result of the declining industrial base, a falling share going into exports. Hence government spending and public employment, they argue, bear a major part of the blame for the slow productivity growth and chronic balance of trade deficits of the British economy. However useful are the social services, however crucial is the welfare state to 'civilised life', it constitutes an unproductive burden on the productive marketed sector of the economy. The growth of the welfare state acts as a brake on the rate of accumulation.

THE 'SOCIAL WAGE'

These analyses, which it must be stressed differ in so many other ways, have one thing in common—they ignore the 'return flow' of state benefits and services back to the capitalist or marketed sector. Since we are here concerned with the welfare state, we shall look at the flow of welfare benefits in cash and in kind back to the employed and non-employed population. This is increasingly referred to as the 'social wage', and government ministers are now prone to compare the value of this social wage with the private and personal wage earned from labour. According to Mr Healey in his April 1975 Budget speech, the social wage was then worth the equivalent of £1000 for every adult member of the working population in the United Kingdom.[9]

Let us therefore begin by drawing together the flows of taxes and social benefits between the state and all 'households' in the economy. Table 6.1 presents an estimate of these flows for the United Kindom in 1975, showing how the original receipt of personal incomes in that year was modified by the actions of the welfare state. In a sense it pulls together the data on expenditure and taxation presented in Chapter 5 and shows its aggregate effect on the 'average household'. It does not discriminate between households which receive their income from labour, from those whose income stems from property or from the state benefits themselves. This is tackled later. One other very important point should be noted: our analysis is entirely static. We simply observe who actually pays the

TABLE 6.1 *Flows between the personal and state sectors in 1975*

£ billion	Personal sector	State sector
Income from employment	60.0	
Income from self-employment	8.7	
Income from property	2.1	
Total personal income	70.8	
Income tax	−15.6 ⟶	+15.6
National insurance contributions	−2.8 ⟶	+2.8
Social-security benefits and other transfers	+9.4 ⟵	−9.4
Disposable incomes	61.8	
Net savings*	−0.3	
Consumption expenditure	61.6	
Indirect taxes	−10.8 ⟶	+10.8
Subsidies	+3.2 ⟵	−3.2
Real consumption	54.0	
Social services in kind	+11.4 ⟵	−11.4
Private and 'social' consumption	65.4	
Net transfers	−5.2	+5.2

NOTES This table attempts to exclude from the CSO's definition of the personal sector (*i*) private non-profit making bodies, such as universities, and (*ii*) life assurance and superannuation funds. Inevitably it provides only a rough estimate.
* This is the difference between two very substantial flows, notably of pension fund and life assurance contributions on the one hand, and the paying out of occupational pensions and assurance policies on the other hand.
SOURCE CSO, *National Income and Expenditure 1965–75*, Tables 4.1, 4.5, 4.7.

taxes and who actually receives the benefits, without enquiring into the indirect impact of these in the longer run. In fact, only a dynamic approach based on class conflict, I shall argue, enables us to understand the impact of growing welfare expenditure, but this is a necessary preliminary step in understanding that process.

Tracing the flows from the top of Table 6.1, we can see how taxes and social-security contributions are deducted from personal incomes, but social-security benefits are paid back to specific households. The result is a net flow of £9 billion from the personal sector to the state. Households then make certain savings from their disposable incomes and receive back the proceeds of past savings, notably pensions and life assurances.[10]

The third stage of the process begins when households spend their remaining income to purchase consumer goods and services. In the process they pay to the state very substantial sums of money in expenditure taxes, particularly on certain goods, and they also pay local-authority rates. As a result the prices of most goods and services are higher than they would otherwise be. On the other hand, certain goods, notably food, housing and transport, are subsidised so that their prices are below market levels. The net result is a further flow of £7.6 billion to the state, and this means that the real value of personal consumption is that much less than actual expenditure. However, state welfare services consist of more than simply cash benefits and subsidies; they also comprise social services in kind, such as education, health services and personal social services. The fourth stage in Table 6.1 shows the value of this return flow of 'collective consumption' expenditure. It is not intended to imply that all such services can be regarded as an unambiguous addition to households' living standards or as part of their 'social wage'. Undeniably, some such services contain elements of a controlling or policing function which should not be regarded as consumption expenditure. The total cost of these services is included merely as an illustration of this important component of welfare expenditure. Nevertheless there is some validity in the notion of a social wage augmenting the private wage, a question discussed in more detail later in this section.

Thus the modern welfare state intervenes at several stages from the initial receipt of incomes, whether from work or property or both. (We have not, of course, discussed the many ways in which it attempts to modify initial incomes.) The net financial result of this state intervention in 1975 was a flow of £5 billion from the personal sector to the state. This contributed to the cost of other items of state expenditure, on arms, infra-structure and, most notably at this time, on aid to the capitalist sector of the economy. It should be noted that 1975 was highly unusual in that the state borrowing requirement was very great. In past years the net taxation of households by the state has been considerably higher as a proportion of initial incomes. In this way the state has transferred substantially more from the personal sector than it has transferred back via the welfare state, a practice found almost universally in advanced capitalist countries according to a recent OECD report.[11]

Despite this, Table 6.1 shows the great importance of the 'social wage' in the United Kingdom today. Ignoring subsidies, the social services in cash and in kind amounted to almost £21 billion in 1975, approaching 30 per cent of personal incomes. It might be thought that this would substantially redistribute incomes from the wealthy to the poor and those in need, but government estimates show that such 'vertical' redistribution is relatively small scale. Table 6.2 summarises the results of a recent official estimate in such a way that the redistributive impact can be compared at each stage of the process in Table 6.1. In order to isolate the vertical element in the redistribution process it considers only one household type—families consisting of a couple and two children.

The first section shows that income taxation and social-security benefits are 'progressive', that is the taxes increase as a share of income as it rises, and the benefits fall, whereas national insurance contributions are 'regressive'. The overall effect is a moderate redistribution of disposable incomes, the lowest income group gaining nothing in the aggregate from the process, whereas the highest group has lost 17 per cent of its original income. When these incomes are spent, however, the incidence of the indirect taxes, including rates, then paid is highly regressive, though the benefits of council-house subsidies flow on the whole to the lowest income groups. The net result at this stage is a reduction in the real consumption levels of all groups and a marked diminution in the redistribution achieved. It is at the third stage, the provision of benefits in kind, that the greatest degree of redistribution is obtained, particularly through the NHS. In the case of education the money value of the education received increases with family income, but as a percentage its relative importance still diminishes somewhat. The overall conclusion is that the massive growth of social expenditure and the concomitant taxation brings about some small vertical redistribution in contemporary Britain. The last two lines show that the initial range of incomes shown in Table 6.2 is 4.5:1 and is reduced at the end of this process to 3.2 : 1. Moreover, if the social services in kind are excluded there is very little redistribution at all. On the other hand, countries raising a greater share of finance from social-security contributions (even if wage-related) or indirect taxes, without subsidies for housing or other necessities and without a national health service would, on the evidence of this study, redistribute income still less, if at all, between income groups.

Other material in this government study shows that the welfare state is primarily an agency for redistributing income 'horizontally' between families of different types and in different situations. Broadly speaking, it channels resources towards families with children,

TABLE 6.2 *Vertical redistribution in 1973*
(within two-adult, two-child households)

	Range of original income (£ per annum)								All (including incomes not separately shown)
% of original income added or subtracted by	987–	1194–	1446–	1949–	2116–	2561–	3099–	3750+	
1. Income tax and surtax	−3	−5	−5	−8	−10	−12	−13	−16	−12
2. Employees' NI contributions	−7	−6	−5	−5	−5	−4	−4	−3	−4
3. Social-security benefits	+12	+7	+8	+4	+3	+2	+2	+1	+3
Gives									
4. Disposable income (%)	101	96	98	91	88	86	85	83	87
5. Indirect taxes	−34	−29	−23	−19	−19	−17	−15	−14	−17
6. Housing subsidies	+14	+8	+5	+3	+3	+2	+1	–	+2

Gives

7. Real personal consumption (%)	81	75	80	75	72	71	71	69	72
8. Education	+12	+9	+10	+10	+9	+8	+8	+6	+8
9. NHS and welfare foods	+14	+12	+10	+8	+7	+5	+4	+3	+5

Gives

10. Income after all taxes and benefits (%)	107	96	100	93	88	84	83	77	86

£ per annum

Original income	1108	1322	1619	1960	2351	2804	3377	5014	2755
Income after all taxes and benefits	1192	1275	1621	1814	2064	2366	2806	3851	2359

SOURCE CSO, *Economic Trends* (December 1974), Appendix IV, Table 1.

pensioner households and the sick. In other words, the welfare state redistributes income *within* the wage- and salary-earning class (the working class, broadly conceived), not from the upper and upper-middle classes downwards, and certainly not necessarily from profits to wage incomes. This is in a context where the net effect of state policies is to direct very substantial sums in the post-war epoch away from the personal sector as a whole towards the corporate sector.

Now let us return to the concepts of Marxist political economy and consider the implications of the foregoing. Tables 6.1 and 6.2, being based on official statistics, treat the whole personal sector as a homogeneous unit and do not distinguish the major social classes within it. Nor do they distinguish the two aspects of the welfare state drawn in Chapter 3—the reproduction of labour power or the employed working population, and the maintenance of the non-working population. Figure 6.1 separates out these two groups and presents a more realistic view of the redistributive activities of the welfare state.[12] (It would be tempting to estimate the values of each of the flows, but that would require a considerable amount of extra work.)

If we ignore the capitalist class and the self-employed, we can divide the population into the employed and the non-working. The reproduction of labour power involves, in quantitative terms, the consumption of the employed population (or the working class broadly conceived). However, as Marx noted, this involves not only the *daily* reproduction of the worker, but also the *generational* reproduction of his/her family and children.[13] Hence the left-hand side of Figure 6.1 includes the families of the working population. The non-working population includes the elderly retired, the long-term sick and handicapped and other groups on the fringes of the labour market. As we noted in Chapter 1, the distinction is not at all clear cut, and part of the non-working population forms part of the industrial reserve army referred to by Marx. Nevertheless, we can divide the two groups in principle and, when this is done, the dual role of the modern welfare state is readily visible.

Broadly speaking it taxes the working population both directly and indirectly as we have already seen. The non-working groups rarely pay income taxes, but they are taxed indirectly when they purchase consumption goods, which complicates the picture slightly. Part of this tax revenue is then returned to working-class families in

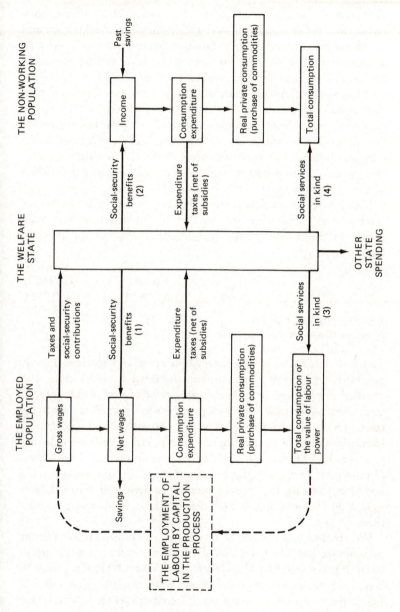

FIGURE 6.1

the form of social-security benefits, for example family allowances, sickness and unemployment benefit to maintain labour power when out of work for short periods, and also in the form of education and health services utilised by these families. But another part, probably a larger part, is channelled to the various non-working groups in the form of old-age pensions, invalidity benefits, health and personal social services etc. A third part, as we have seen, remains to be spent by the state on other items, chiefly to the direct benefit of the capitalist sector. Viewed in these static terms, it follows that the return flow of welfare benefits to secure the reproduction of labour power falls far short of the taxes extracted from the working class. A considerable portion goes to maintain the non-working population and to secure the reproduction of capital.

It also helps us to define more precisely what we mean by the 'social wage'. The social services can be divided into four main groups in the following way (the numbers refer to the flows in Figure 6.1):

	Services to employed population	Services to non-working population
Benefits in cash—social wage	1	2
Benefits in kind—collective consumption	3	4

The first distinction is between cash benefits and services directly provided by the state. Cash benefits augment money income and are used to purchase *commodities*. State-provided services are directly consumed as *use values*: no money payment is made as with the consumption of commodities. For this reason it may be preferable to restrict the term 'social wage' to the group of cash benefits and call the benefits in kind 'collective consumption'. The second distinction is between those benefits received by the working class and thus entering the reproduction of present and future labour power, and those supporting the dependent or non-working population.

We are now in a position to return to the problem outlined in the previous section. The belief that all taxes are deductions from surplus value implies that the remainder—the value of labour power—is conceived net of all taxes and of all state benefits. The value of labour power thus refers to the actual commodities purchased by the worker and his/her family out of wages. But immediately two problems are encountered. First, part of these goods and services are purchased with social-security benefits, and it makes no sense to separate off the loaf of bread bought with the family allowance from that bought with the wage packet. Secondly, in terms of the use value consumed in the course of reproducing labour power, an increasing portion of them are now provided directly by the state and are not purchased at all by the family. Yet these services contribute to the daily and generational reproduction of the working class in just the same way as commodities. If they are excluded from the value of labour power, it is clear that the latter is progressively diverging from its original definition—the total labour necessary to reproduce the worker and his/her family. It makes more sense, therefore, to hold on to this concept and include the labour which produces consumption goods and services in both the capitalist *and* the state sector of the economy. The value of labour power is thus measured by the private *and* collective consumption of the employed population in capitalist economies.[14]

In this way, we can observe the operations depicted within Figure 6.1 as all occurring within the value of labour power. There is no necessity, therefore, to assume that the growth of the welfare state will inevitably reduce the quantity of surplus value in the capitalist sector and thus inhibit accumulation and growth. Instead, one can argue that a greater share of wage and salary income is channelled via the state, some to return to working families, some to the dependent population and some to finance other areas of state expenditure. This redistribution of payments for labour need not necessarily encroach on the share of profits or surplus value in total output. But this is to jump ahead of our argument. Before we can fully answer this question we need to take up two further points. First, what is the nature and impact of state-produced services and, second, what are the dynamic implications of a growing welfare state? These questions occupy the remaining sections of this chapter.

THE PRODUCTION OF SOCIAL SERVICES

It is time to focus our attention on the 'collective consumption' item noted above: the direct state production of welfare services, such as education, school meals, health services, personal social services and so forth. As we noted in Chapter 5, these lay claim to real resources in the form of labour, equipment and raw materials that would otherwise be available for the capitalist sector. Put another way, part of the labour power reproduced in the capitalist mode of production today is directly employed by the state to produce use values which in turn aid the further reproduction of labour power. In the last section we considered only the *distributional* impact of the welfare state; it is time now to analyse its growing role in *production* and the effect of this on the capitalist sector of the economy. This section is inevitably more difficult than the others, however, and some readers may prefer to proceed straight to the next.

We noted in Chapter 5 (Table 5.4) that the civilian population employed by central and local government in the United Kingdom (excluding the armed forces and public corporations) totalled 4.6 million in 1974, or 18 per cent of the total labour force. This labour was not available for employment in the marketed or productive sector of the economy, as we have defined it. The rapid growth in public employment over the last few years, therefore, means that the ratio of unproductive to productive labour has increased. As Bacon and Eltis argue, this labour not only has to be paid for, by taxes or some other means (this characteristic it shares with all government expenditure except for the nationalised industries), but it directly reduces the potential output of the productive or marketed sector. Labour that could have been employed by capital, producing surplus value and profits, is now employed by the state producing neither. Let us consider this argument more carefully.

The fact that the National Health Service does not generate profits does not mean, of course, that health services are not produced and consumed. They are produced and consumed directly as use values, instead of in the form of commodities to be sold and bought. Let us suppose that if there were no NHS the population would purchase the same amount of health services, and let us further assume that the NHS is entirely financed from taxes levied on the personal sector. In this case the socialisation of health services means that the entire personal sector pays more out in the form of taxes but needs to purchase less in the form of commodities. The net effect on the personal sector as a whole will be zero, as the rising taxes to pay for the health services are offset by the reduced expenditure on private health insurance and the like. Does this therefore mean that the value of labour power and hence the total quantity of surplus value is unaffected by the introduction of a socialised health service? Can this be so, if beforehand private capital was operating in the health sphere producing surplus value and profits?

The answer to this question is not at all simple. Rowthorn[15] has pointed out that, under certain conditions, state employees too will perform surplus labour, analogous to the surplus value performed by productive workers. That is, they will work for a greater amount of time than the labour time embodied in the commodities (wage goods) they consume. Given free movement of labour between the state and capitalist sectors, the rate of exploitation between the two will tend to be equalised. Now this means there is a net flow of 'labour time' embodied in goods and services from the state to the personal sector in the following manner. The taxes levied on this sector will pay for state purchases (social constant capital—C) and the necessary or paid labour of the state workers (social variable capital—V). But the services provided will incorporate the value of $C + V$ plus the unpaid or surplus labour of state workers—S. In the case of social services like education and health the use values consumed by workers and their families will embody the surplus or unpaid labour of teachers, doctors, nurses and so on. (This is elaborated in Appendix C.)

This can be illustrated by comparing state-produced health services with privately-produced services. In the latter case the family, laying out money to purchase the service, pays for the profits of the health capitalist, just as in the purchase, of any wage good. The money laid out corresponds to the labour time performed in producing the service ($= C + V + S$). Now suppose that the health service is nationalised and provided 'free'. It has to be financed of course—we have supposed by taxes levied on and paid by the working class.

Since there is no capitalist to appropriate the labour of health workers, the service can be supplied 'at cost'. The taxes need cover only the means of production plus the labour of the health workers ($C + V$) so the family clearly gains by comparison with purchasing privately-produced health services. The form of payment will have changed, but the extra taxes are more than compensated for by the reduced private health insurance premiums etc. In this example, labour's gain is capital's loss as the profits of the health industry no longer exist. Note that this conclusion holds even though labour bears the entire cost in the form of increased taxes.

However, if following this change, capital can reduce the wages paid to workers, or increase them at a slower rate than it would otherwise have done, then it may be able to appropriate part or all of this gain. In this case the surplus labour of health workers will appear in the form of extra profits for capital. Here the loss of the health capitalists will be the gain of the rest of the capitalist sector and total profits in the economy will be unaffected. Even so the issues are not yet entirely settled. First, whether or not state employees perform surplus labour and whether or not this augments profits in the capitalist sector, the fact is that in a situation of full employment the state is competing for labour with the capitalist sector. This will either produce shortages of the necessary types of labour, or will bid up wages, or both, and in all cases surplus value and profits will be reduced (*ceteris paribus*). This is the nub of the de-industrialisation process, according to Bacon and Eltis. Nonetheless, as they recognise and as others have demonstrated, much of the growth of personnel in the social services in the United Kingdom has come from new entrants to the labour market, in particular married women. According to Klein, for example, the number of full-time men working for British local authorities increased by 13 per cent from 1964 to 1974, whilst the number of part-time women rose by one-third of a million—an increase of no less than 86 per cent.[16] The nature of service employment, the unskilled nature of many ancillary jobs and other factors may mean, therefore, that the social services do not directly drain labour away from the 'marketed' sector. On the contrary, they draw in new, predominantly female, labour from the 'reserve army' (a phenomenon not without further implications for the operation of capitalist economies).

A second problem with the analysis presented above is that it assumes all social services are 'wage goods', that is services that would otherwise be purchased by working families. This is clearly untrue in at least two ways. First, a substantial part of welfare services are directed towards the non-working population, hence do not re-enter the value of labour power, as illustrated in Figure 6.1. Services for the mentally ill or the elderly utilise state power to redirect resources away from the working population. Yet here, too, if they reduce the burdens on working families who would otherwise support their relatives, the net effect on the value of labour power or real wages may not be so great. Undoubtedly part of the growth of these services reflects a growing inability or unwillingness on the part of working families to shoulder all these burdens.[17]

The second proviso is more problematic and refers to the 'social control' aspects of the welfare state. By no means can all welfare services be regarded as simply wage goods, or 'social consumption' to use O'Connor's term, that is 'projects and services that lower the reproduction costs of labour power'. Some he included in the category of 'social expenses', that is projects and services which are required to maintain harmony or to secure legitimacy.[18] This brings us back to the division of state-produced services between social investment, social consumption and social expenses, elaborated in Chapter 3. Some further implications of this three-fold division of state activity are considered in Appendix B, and here I wish merely to summarise some important conclusions.

As O'Connor notes, it is extremely difficult to classify any activity in this way, since nearly every state expenditure is part social investment, part social consumption and part social expense. Most welfare services fall into the last two categories and it would be none too easy to determine their relative weights. Insofar as the services contribute to the reproduction of the working population or alter the attributes of present and future labour power, they would constitute social consumption. Insofar as they maintain other groups in the population, or form part of the agencies of social control and coercion within society, they are a social expense. The problems lie in the last category. Probation services and parts of social work may be regarded as a cost of maintaining social harmony, but so are certain aspects of the education and health systems. State-subsidised housing may contribute to the reproduction of labour power, but part may be utilised by non-working groups in the population. Nonetheless, our interpretation of the welfare state as a unity of these two components means that we must at a theoretical level make the distinction. Assuming this can be done, what is its relevance for our concerns in this chapter?

It means that we can divide the social services between the *reproductive* and the *non-reproductive*. (The same can be done with capitalist sector output, as is demonstrated in Appendix B.) The former contribute to the reproduction of labour power and thus enter into the variable capital of society. This variable capital then re-enters the production process to produce further output. The activity of these state workers can therefore be appropriated either by private capital or by labour. Non-reproductive state services on the other hand are part of the social costs of maintaining social relations or 'social harmony'. They do not enter into the production of future labour power (variable capital) or means of production (constant capital). They are simply a social expense borne by capital or labour: the larger is this expense, the greater is the amount of total social labour time 'wasted' from the point of view of the capitalist system. In other words the smaller is the army, or the civil service, or the police force, or the myriad other agents of social control, the greater is the quantum of capital available for the production of use values that ensure future reproduction. This is seen most clearly in wartime when vastly expanded military production depletes the output of means of production and wage goods and thereby reduces the productive potential of the economy in the longer term.

Returning to the welfare state, it follows that the division of services between 'social consumption' and 'social expenses' has important implications for the long-term accumulation of capital. The more social services contribute to the reproduction of labour power (in qualitative and quantitative terms) the more they contribute to the long-term production of output. If these state workers at the same time perform surplus labour they will also contribute to profits and/or real wages in the capitalist sector. The more that social welfare *expenses* grow, on the other hand, the less is available for future output. Much more work is required on the balance between these two components of the welfare state and their growth in recent years.

CLASS CONFLICT, TAXATION AND SOCIAL EXPENDITURE

In the real world of capitalism there is continual conflict between capital and labour. This can take a variety of forms: economic (over the shares of profits and wages in national output, over the conditions and intensity of the work process), political (over state policies, government expenditure, taxation and, nowadays more and more, over prices and incomes too), and ideological (over amongst other things the goals of social and economic policies). The rise of the interventionist state has added to and in some cases transformed this underlying conflict between capital and labour. So too has the growth of professional associations, self-employed groups and the numerous other pressure groups within advanced capitalist societies, but this has not altered the fundamental dichotomy within these societies. It is time now to introduce this ongoing class conflict into our previous analysis, to make it less abstract. At the same time I shall try to integrate some of the points made earlier on in Chapters 4 and 5.

In Chapter 4 it was argued that the overall nature and level of social spending and of state expenditure as a whole reflected two major factors:

(*i*) the requirement of the capitalist economy as mediated by the state structure and state policies;
(*ii*) the class balance of forces within capitalist society.

In this chapter it has been argued that the effect of growing social expenditure depends on its type (whether transfers, purchases or state-produced services), its nature (the department of production or, in the case of transfers, the class to which it is directed), the manner in which it is financed and the final incidence of taxes. These factors in turn will be determined by

(*i*) the requirements of capital accumulation, and the relations of production;
(*ii*) the class balance of forces.

In both cases, therefore, we need to consider these two issues in order to progress further. A brief outline of my view of the post-war period, in the advanced capitalist world as a whole and in Britain in particular, was given in Chapter 4. My purpose here is to situate our analysis of social and other state expenditure within that framework.[19]

The capitalist system in the post-war period experienced an unprecedented expansion. It expanded both in width, drawing on the labour reserves within the advanced countries and outside them; and in depth, drawing on the previous stock of technology, chiefly in the United States. It was aided by the hegemony of the United States and the dependence of the Third World which enabled the advanced countries to reap the benefits of favourable terms of trade. This rapid rate of accumulation and growth had in turn two important effects. First, the reserve army of labour was rapidly depleted within the advanced countries, resulting in labour shortages and a strengthening of the labour movement.[20] Second, the range of state functions and expenditure increased, for the reasons outlined in Chapter 4. In the short term, by raising demand these effects added to the cumulative process of growth. The period from the early 1950s to the early 1970s saw a remarkable revival of a previously flagging capitalist system. It also witnessed the golden age of the welfare state.

However, all these causes of the long boom contained within them the seeds of their own destruction. (This is precisely what is meant by saying that a process is contradictory.) The rest of the advanced world eventually 'caught up' with US levels of technology; the exhaustion of accessible raw materials drove up their prices and worsened terms of trade; the United States was increasingly challenged by the growing power of European and Japanese capitalism.

Furthermore, and more important for our purposes, the very dynamism of capital accumulation, by exhausting the reserve army of labour within the central countries, strengthened the labour movements economically within them. (It does not follow automatically that their political influence on the state grew, however.) Both factors, the slow-down in growth and greater working-class strength, reacted back on the level and direction of state expenditure. More powerful labour movements were able to raise the share of wages and decrease that of profits and, via growing organisations at the point of production in the form of shop stewards systems, probably braked the growth of productivity in certain sectors. In turn, rising state expenditure exacerbated the underlying conflict between capital and labour.

Lastly, the end of the long boom and the onset of crisis laid further demands on the state, increasing its expenditure in the economic field (the restructuring of industry, aid to the private sector etc.) and the social field (unemployment costs, retraining and youth employment schemes etc.).

All these features were present in greater force within British capitalism. The low rate of economic growth throughout the post-war period reflected a seriously weakened economy relative to its major competitors. The post-war unity and strength of the labour movement and the earlier achievement of full employment meant that the decline in profits began sooner, in the early 1960s.

Both the low productivity growth and the heightened conflict (in the field of production and distribution) exacerbated Britain's economic weakness and resulted in growing intervention by the state. In the 1960s there coincided a rapid expansion of state spending on both economic services and social services. The state, seeking to restructure industry and increase its competitiveness, introduced investment grants, founded the Industrial Reorganisation Corporation, extended infrastructure investment (for example motorways) and so forth. At the same time the labour movement succeeded in extracting from the state a greater priority to renewing outdated social capital, improving social services and raising social-security benefits. The result of this was a growing problem of financing this expenditure: the 'fiscal crisis of the state'. Let us analyse this in more detail and relate it back to the welfare state by focusing on the finance of this state expenditure. Broadly speaking, within this context all attempts to finance a growing level of government spending will either fuel inflation, or reduce profits, investment and accumulation, or both.

To understand this, let us place ourselves in the position of the Chancellor of the Exchequer or his equivalent in the last few years, attempting to finance the growth in state expenditure. (It may be helpful to refer back to Table 6.1 when reading the following.) The options open to him are as follows:

(*i*) To raise direct taxes on households. This will reduce take-home pay or net wages. If gross wages are not raised to compensate for this, it could permit the state to offer further tax concessions and economic aid to the capitalist sector, increasing the profits share. If at the same time the state attempts to restructure British industry and direct these funds towards the centres of accumulation, growth could also be encouraged. But the very strength of the labour movement has prevented such an option several times in the past. If direct *political* pressure does not forestall this increased taxation, then the *economic* power of the trade unions can be utilised to secure a rise in money wages sufficient to offset the higher taxes. If this is passed on in terms of higher prices, inflation will accelerate; if it is not, profits will decline.

(*ii*) To raise direct taxes on the capitalist sector. Again this will either fuel inflationary pressures and reduce competitiveness (if they are passed on in the form of higher prices), or reduce profits and investment (if they are absorbed by firms).

(*iii*) To raise indirect taxes. Taxes on expenditure directly increase prices and thus fuel inflation. If the taxed goods and services are predominantly wage goods, this raises the cost of living and exacerbates the pressure for higher wages to offset it. If the taxes fall on inputs, they raise costs and reduce competitiveness in the economy. The same argument applies to a policy of reducing subsidies on food or to the nationalised industries.

(*iv*) To increase state borrowing. If this is not absorbed by the personal or company sectors, it will increase the supply of money and thus add to inflationary pressures. If it results in a parallel reduction in private-sector expenditure this may not occur, but other problems ensue. If it is absorbed by the personal sector, that is real savings increase, then real consumption levels will fall. (This might be brought about anonymously by means of large pension-fund surpluses which are invested in government stock.) Again, though, the end result is a reduction in net pay with the consequences analysed in (*i*) above. If it is company saving that is increased, then the government borrowing may seriously diminish funds available for investment in the capitalist sector.

Twist and turn as he may, the Chancellor cannot escape this Catch-22 situation except by altering one or more of the basic parameters. Given a low level of productivity growth and the ability of labour to protect real wage levels, it is impossible to finance this growing level of state expenditure in a way that does not worsen inflation or growth or both. This conclusion holds despite the analysis of the previous section which demonstrated the indirectly productive nature of much state expenditure. There, much depended on ensuring that the ultimate burden of financing this would fall on the working class. If the cost of the welfare state *could* be borne by the household sector, predominantly the broad working class, then its expansion would not necessarily harm surplus value and capital accumulation. But this is one extreme case. On the other hand, the opposite situation, where all taxes are ultimately borne by capital and thus reduce remaining surplus value, is an equally unlikely one.

In the real world the final burden of taxation is determined by the ebb and flow of class conflict, and will vary with the economic and political strength of the contending classes. Simultaneously the scale and direction of state expenditure, including that on the social services, is also largely influenced by the class balance of forces.

But this situation is problematic for the future of capitalist economies because the outcome of this conflict is the chronic inflation of the post-war world. The instabilities that this has generated have brought about the contemporary economic crisis and a marked slow-down in the rate of capital accumulation and economic growth.

The growth of the welfare state is neither cause nor consequence of capitalist development, but one aspect of it. Consequently it is neither cause nor consequence of the present crisis, but again one aspect of it. The ever-growing level of state impositions and welfare expenditures exacerbates the conflict between capital and labour in the economic, political and ideological spheres. The combination of upward pressures on welfare spending and the problems of financing it result in what O'Connor refers to as 'the fiscal crisis of the state'. But this can only be understood as one moment in the present economic crisis, brought about by the very nature of capitalist growth and development.

7

THE WELFARE STATE
AND THE CRISIS

The growth in the welfare state here and abroad came to an abrupt end in the mid-1970s. Public expenditure was cut back and, within this total, social expenditure suffered the most. The process began in Britain with the cuts in planned future expenditure announced in May and December 1973, which together lopped off £1700 million from expenditure in 1974/5, of which about £400 million was from social-service spending. The White Paper on Public Expenditure published in January 1975 reduced the planned growth in several programmes, but the overall trend was still upward. Shortly afterwards, however, the Chancellor announced in his budget statement in April 1975 a further cut in planned expenditure of £1.1 billion for 1976/7, of which about £335 million fell on the social services. The 1976 White Paper, published in February, sharply reduced planned growth from 1977/8 onwards but raised it somewhat for 1976/7. There then followed two more rounds of substantial cuts in July and December 1976 totalling £2 billion, which for the first time planned an absolute drop in total state spending in 1977/8 and the following year.[1] The official aim, according to the 1977 White Paper, 'The Government's Expenditure Plans', was to reduce the total share of state expenditure in GNP up to the end of the decade. Using the Treasury's new method of computing public expenditure, it was forecast to fall (as a percentage of GDP at factor cost) from $51\frac{1}{2}$ per cent in 1975/6 to 48 per cent in 1978/79.[2]

Because the price basis changes, because rates of increase are expressed on different expenditure out-turns (and sometimes on future planned levels), and for many other reasons, it is notoriously difficult to pin down the effect of these increases on actual spending levels. Table 7.1 summarises the evidence on the turn-around which took place in the mid-1970s. It shows the rate of increase in different categories of expenditure for three two-year periods: 1971–3, 1973–5 and 1975–7. The first two are actual past rates of increase, the last is the projected trend announced in the January 1977 White Paper. (All refer to financial years, running from 1 April to 31 March, so that 1975/7 refers to financial year 1977/8 compared with 1975/6.)

The picture which results is a dramatic one. If we look first at total social-service spending (including food subsidies) it increased from 1971 to 1973 by 12 per cent (that is, 6 per cent per annum average) and from 1973 to 1975 by 14 per cent (7 per cent per annum average). The projected change for the two years 1975–7 is −1 per cent. The switch from +14 per cent to −1 per cent is a measure of the reversal in the post-war trend which took place in 1975. Bearing in mind 'automatic' factors, the adverse effects of the economic crisis and the steady growth in needs, all of which necessitate a year-by-year *increase* in expenditure simply to stand still, it is apparent that the level and quality of many social services must have fallen. This was explicitly recognised in the 1977 White Paper which referred to the 'closure of hospitals' and rising staff–student ratios in education. So far, though, it would appear that the social-service labour force has not yet fallen, and any shedding of labour has taken the form of 'natural wastage' rather than redundancies.

The cutback in welfare spending is more marked than for state spending as a whole because its previous growth rate was higher. Within this total there are sharp differences. Social security was planned to rise steadily in 1975–7 and, since this is the largest single item, the other social services are affected more than the overall total would suggest. The burden fell mainly on food subsidies (which were rapidly phased out), housing, education and, above all, on the personal social services. These have expanded rapidly in recent years, and the switch from 17 per cent growth in 1973–5 to 11 per cent contraction in 1975–7 is dramatic.

Also important is the division between current and capital spending (see Table 7.1, centre section). Capital spending on the social services rose rapidly in the early 1970s but was sharply cut back in 1974. 1973–5 might be termed *phase 1* of the cuts when capital projects were severely cut back but current spending continued to rise, in fact accelerated. *Phase 2* began in 1976, when for the first time the

TABLE 7.1   *The 'cuts' in social expenditure (% change over two-year periods at 1976 prices (excluding the relative price effect))*

	Financial years		
	1971–3	*1973–5* cuts— phase 1	*1975–7* *(projected)* cuts—phase 2
Total social services	+12	+11	+ 1
Total including food subsidies	+12	+14	− 1
Personal social services	+32	+17	−11
Health services	+ 9	+ 4	+ 2
Education	+12	+ 3	− 2
Social security	+ 5	+16	+ 8
Housing	+36	+24	− 7
*Total public expenditure**	+ 8	+10	− 1
Current v. Capital:			
Current: personal social services	+28	+25	+ 6
health	+ 8	+ 7	+ 5
education	+12	+ 9	+ 1
Total current (including all other items)	+ 6	+ 8	+ 1
Capital: personal social services	+59	−25	−54
health	+17	−15	−28
education	+10	−28	−36
Total capital (including all other items)	+10	− 3	−22
Central v. Local:			
Total central government	+ 4	+13	− 3
Total local government	+15	+ 8	− 9

* Including investment grants and debt interest (new basis).
SOURCE   Cmnd. 6721: *The Government's Expenditure Plans*, 2 vols.

rise in current spending was almost halted even in the most labour-intensive social services, whilst capital spending was further reduced from its already low levels. By 1977/8, for example, capital spending in education and the personal social services amounted to less than one-half the level in 1973/4.

Lastly, Table 7.1 shows the respective impact of the cuts on central and local expenditure. The latter's share rose during the late 1960s and early 1970s but this was reversed from 1973 onwards, when the major transfer items, for which Whitehall is responsible, expanded. Phase 2 of the cuts widened the gap, particularly in the social services, as the three services which dominate local government—education, housing and social welfare—were drastically pruned back. The major mechanism for achieving this was the institution of cash limits. By 1976/7, two-thirds of voted expenditure was subject to a planned ceiling in cash terms on the extent to which initial estimates could be raised by supplementary votes, and this included the crucial Rate Support Grant.

At the same time that most areas of expenditure were being cut back, certain items continued to expand, for instance expenditure on police, nationalised industry investment (particularly in the energy field), aid to the private sector (for example the National Enterprise Board) and debt interest. What we are witnessing is not so much a *cut* in total state spending (the doubling of government net interest payments from 1975/6 to 1977/8 will see to that) but its *restructuring* in specific directions. Broadly speaking, this continues a trend begun in the late 1960s of increasing state intervention in the restructuring of private capital to enable it to respond to the international economic crisis.

> Within total public expenditure, a higher priority is being given to expenditure which is designed to maintain or improve our industrial capability.[3]

This process of restructuring extends to the welfare state—an important point elaborated in the next section.

The pattern of cuts and restructuring of public expenditure is by no means peculiar to Britain: it is a general feature of the advanced capitalist world. In West Germany, the Budget Structure Act of 1975 raised unemployment insurance contributions and cut expenditure on education, hospitals and other items. In the United States the near-bankruptcy of New York City in 1975 dramatically highlighted the fiscal crisis of US cities and the unwillingness of the Federal Government to undertake radical measures to help them. Many public employees there have been sacked: in New York City alone, 60,000 were laid off between 1975 and 1977, and the number of municipal workers in the United States as a whole fell for the first time in 1976 by 1.7 per cent.[4]

The cuts in expenditure, especially on the welfare state, here and abroad are evidently related to the unprecedented crisis of the world capitalist economy. From the end of 1973 right through to 1975 it experienced a slump unparalleled since before the war. The combined GNP of the OECD countries fell by 5 per cent, industrial output plummeted, and world trade declined by 14 per cent. Unemployment climbed to a staggering 15 million in all OECD countries combined. At the same time, inflation accelerated and the advanced capitalist world experienced a growing collective trade deficit. For the weaker economies, such as Britain, the slump, though it arrived later, has been more prolonged. By 1977, British GDP was still below the 1973/4 level, industrial production was barely above 1970 levels, industrial investment was down to 80 per cent of 1974 levels. Annual inflation rates peaked at 26 per cent in 1975 but in 1977 still hovered around 16 per cent, whilst unemployment continued to rise to an unprecedented 1.6 million in August 1977. Personal disposable incomes remained stagnant for four years and for the average wage-earner were no higher in 1977 than they were in 1970. The only economic index to register an improvement was the balance of payments moving into surplus from the record trade deficit of 1974. At the same time, investment remained sluggish throughout 1977 and the outlook for economic growth was poor. By this time the 'strong' capitalist economies (the United States, Japan and Germany) were beginning to reflate but at a rate quite insufficient to pull the world economy out of the mire of depression. Underlying the halt to accumulation on a world scale has been the decline in the motor force of capitalist economies: profits. In the United States, West Germany and most notably in the United Kingdom the last decade has witnessed a long-term decline in the profitability of industrial and commercial companies.[5] In real terms the profit rate in Britain fell from 13 per cent in 1960 to 4 per cent in 1975.

In the state sector the yawning gap between expenditure and revenues was the most visible manifestation of the crisis. This gap is known as the public sector borrowing requirement (PSBR) and as the phrase suggests indicates the amount of money that must be borrowed or printed to finance it. It multiplied in the mid-1970s in Britain as Table 5.1 showed, to £6.3 billion or 8½ per cent of GNP in 1974 and to £10.5 billion or 11 per cent of GNP in 1975. By 1976 it had been reduced to £9.5 billion (9 per cent of GNP) and a further fall was predicted for 1977 and 1978. Nevertheless, the accumulated budget deficits of these four years are immense and will generate a substantial burden of interest payments in future years. Again this is not a phenomenon peculiar to Britain, for the slump generated a rise in budget deficits in all countries. In 1976 the PSBR as a percentage of GNP amounted to 10 per cent in Italy, 5¾ per cent in Germany and 4¼ per cent in Japan.

This is not the place to discuss the reaction of Western governments, nor even the British Government, to this unprecedented (in post-war terms) economic crisis. All we shall do here is consider its policies on state and welfare spending, as elaborated in the annual White Paper on Public Expenditure. These do not refer to a crisis (except for the 'energy' crisis) but there is recognition of the original combination of problems facing the British economy. These are:

the large deficit in the balance of payments, the high rate of inflation, and the high level of unemployment. Associated with these problems is a large public sector borrowing requirement, which poses considerable problems for monetary management and industrial financing.[6]

At the same time there was recognition that world-wide recovery from the slump would be slow and halting.

The cuts in public expenditure would help in several ways, the government argued:

The objectives of that plan (the 1976 cuts) were to make possible a shift of resources into industrial investment and exports; to restrain the increase in the burden of taxation which would otherwise have been necessary; to maintain an appropriate balance between take-home pay and the provision of public services; and by these means to help to reduce inflationary pressure in the economy.[7]

So according to the government, the cuts and restructuring of public expenditure would help attack all three problems:

(i) The balance of payments deficit, by releasing resources to be devoted to the private sector with which to generate more exports.
(ii) Inflation, by (a) reducing the PSBR and the inflationary pressures this generates, and (b) permitting a reduction in taxation levels which exacerbate cost inflation.
(iii) Unemployment, by releasing resources for private investment with which to regenerate British industry, economic growth and jobs.

If the arguments are couched in Keynesian terms, the policies are the very antithesis of orthodox Keynesianism, which would recommend increased government spending and budget deficits in order to raise aggregate demand and thus raise output and reduce unemployment. The policies of cutting government spending and economic retrenchment were precisely those attacked by Keynes in the Great Depression of the 1930s. At that time the orthodox Treasury view prevailed and in the midst of a political crisis the dole was cut by 10 per cent. As Fraser puts it:

> The fate of . . . the nation depended on whether an unemployed man should live on 17s a week or 15s 3d.[8]

Now, following almost three decades in which Keynesianism has in turn become the orthodox economic doctrine and commitment to full employment a cardinal principle of political life, it is to be abandoned again. Not only that but the same call for cuts in welfare expenditure have been issued and heeded by the government. Unemployment benefit has not actually been cut, though many benefits have failed to keep pace with price inflation, but spending on housing, education, food subsidies and social welfare has been. The fate of the nation now appears to depend, we might say, on the number of home-helps for the elderly or the price of school meals. One effect of the current 'slumpflation' has thus been a crisis in Keynesian economics itself.

Accordingly, almost all schools of economic thought in Britain today link 'excessive' government spending with some aspect of the economic crisis. The monetarists, of course, are most vociferous here. For them the major problem is the huge government borrowing requirement. This is not necessarily inflationary, it is recognised, if it does not excessively increase the money supply. However, to achieve this would either require very high rates of interest or absorb funds otherwise available for commercial investment.

As a consequence, the budget deficit is financed by printing money or borrowing from the banking system, which expands the money supply and generates inflation.[9] The only answer, they argue, is a substantial cut in public expenditure, if anything an overkill policy which permits personal taxation also to be reduced somewhat. This position is endorsed, implicitly or explicitly, not only by the Conservative Party, which has in Sir Keith Joseph an articulate advocate of the monetarist philosophy, but also by almost all of the national newspapers. From *The Times* to the *Sun*, massive cuts in state spending have been advocated as an essential answer to the crisis. Alongside arguments about the stifling effect of state spending on industrial enterprise, investment and exports, are encountered strong attacks on the 'bloated bureaucracy' of the welfare state, and on welfare scroungers, together with support for IMF intervention and attempts to restore 'foreign confidence'. Many even seemed to think that hardship and sacrifice *per se* were a good thing and would restore the economy:

> The Mirror has News for him [the Chancellor]: people don't want cheering up. They want to take the medicine like adults and get it over with.[10]

But the monetarists are not alone. The influential 'de-industrialisation' thesis of Bacon and Eltis has already been mentioned. The 'New Cambridge School' links budget deficits with balance of payments deficits and argues that public expenditure, especially local-authority spending, is 'out of control'. So that in different, indeed partly contradictory, ways most economic writers today lay part or all of the blame for the current crisis at the door of 'excessive' state spending. All are thus agreed on the need to cut some part of it drastically.

Arguing against this position and in defence of welfare expenditure, at least, are the trade unions, notably those in the public sector, and the Labour Party. Appropriately enough their arguments are primarily based on orthodox Keynesian analysis: that the cuts will reduce demand and raise unemployment as well as reducing the 'social wage' component of the standard of living. This is buttressed by referring to the growing burden placed on the social services by the 'productive' sector of the economy and, in a British context, by observing that levels of total taxation are higher in other countries.[11] Apart from the labour movement, then, the opinion of economic science, government and the press alike is unequivocal. Excessive state expenditure, welfare spending in particular, *is* a major cause of the contemporary economic crisis and must be cut.

Our own view of the crisis, not by any means the only one within current Marxist political economy, has been briefly spelt out in Chapter 6.[12] The seeds of the current world crisis germinated precisely during the preceding 'long boom' of the post-war years. This both exhausted the post-war potential for accumulation and growth within the capitalist world and altered the class balance of forces within the advanced countries. Squeezed between these two sets of forces, the rate of profit has declined and with it the motor force for future growth. The need on the part of capital is to re-establish conditions for profitable accumulation, but the very balance of class forces makes this difficult to achieve unless and until they altered. The term 'crisis' is used here to signify just such a combination of circumstances.[13] For reproduction and accumulation to continue, certain parameters within the advanced capitalist world must be changed, but the current balance of class forces resist such change. It should be pointed out that, even should this occur, the period of re-adjustment would be a very long one, involving changed international relations on a world scale. Current prognoses for the world capitalist economy vary from the gloomy to the disastrous, and nobody expects a flowering of the productive forces such as occurred over the last three decades, at least not for a very long time. As this was also the golden age of the welfare state, the end of this benign economic environment is pregnant with implications for its future.

RESTRUCTURING THE WELFARE STATE

The 'cuts' in social services have formed a major plank in the government's response to the economic crisis, but welfare cuts are by no means an unambiguous benefit to the capitalist system. At the most general level a reduction in the welfare state itself interferes with the reproduction of capitalist societies, not only the reproduction of labour power, but also the maintenance of social integration and harmony and the reproduction of capitalist social relations (see Chapter 3). Let us try and elaborate this in some more detail.

First, the economic crisis itself places new demands on the state services concerned with social control. For example, the growth of youth unemployment has generated a plethora of new schemes directed at this group.[14] In 1977 there were already 2 million young people out of work in the EEC as a whole, and under-nineteen-year-olds made up about 31 per cent of the unemployed in Britain. This poses problems not only of political and social unrest, particularly in the declining conurbations like Liverpool and Glasgow, but of the permanent unemployability of these groups. The result has been a host of schemes designed to draw the young unemployed off the streets and to give them a 'realistic introduction to the requirements, disciplines and satisfactions of working life'.[15] All told, government expenditure on such schemes totalled £900 million between 1975 and 1977, by which time over 300,000 were 'benefiting' from them.[16]

Second, the need to secure an effective labour market may involve still higher levels of spending in present conditions. For example, the overlap of the social-security and personal tax systems in the United Kingdom, alongside low wages in certain occupations, has resulted in 'the poverty trap' and a lack of incentive to work. This inhibits workers or potential workers from adopting 'appropriate labour market behaviour'. Now of course one brutal but simple way of dealing with this problem would be to reduce supplementary benefit and other social benefits, but this is probably politically unacceptable and may in any case generate further problems of social control. Moreover, it is precisely the pursuit of 'cheaper' selective benefits that has caused the poverty trap in the first place. Now it is recognised that a raising of the tax threshold and/or more generous child benefits (so that net income per child in and out of work come more into line) is necessary. Either way the net burden on the Exchequer will increase not decline.

Third, in strictly economic terms the cuts have been extremely harmful to some sections of British industry because the demand for their output has been cut back. The UK construction industry has suffered severely from the cutback in government capital programmes and has been pleading for a restoration of these cuts. This brings us back to the conflict between the *production* and *realisation* of surplus value and profits within capitalism, though both processes must be successfully completed in order for the capitalist class to appropriate surplus value, as Sutcliffe concisely argues:

> The *production* of surplus value depends on the capitalist's ability to manage the workers he employs in such a way that the value of what they produce is greater than the value of what he is forced to pay them in wages. The *realisation* of this surplus value then depends on the capitalist's ability to sell his product in the market at its value. Capitalism is of necessity a unity of these

two processes; and yet the conditions for achieving both of them successfully are in contradiction with each other. The things which make the realisation of surplus value easy simultaneously make the production of surplus value more difficult.[17]

He continues: 'One of these things seems to be state expenditure.'

A high level of state expenditure maintains demand and employment, but may reduce profits and accumulation. Cutting state expenditure to raise the latter may, on the other hand, reduce aggregate demand and employment still further in the short run. For individual sectors of capital, these short-run effects can be catastrophic, as the experience of the construction industry testifies.

These are three examples of the numerous ways in which cuts in the welfare services may harm the long- and short-term interests of capital. Yet it is also true to say that some social expenditure is harmful to capital in other ways, so that cuts here would be welcomed. For example, the long-term trend for social-security benefits (the social wage) to rise as a share of net incomes from work has already been referred to. For many families it is now a rational decision not to seek work, and this will slowly sap the 'work ethic' on which a capitalist economy depends.

In this situation then we would expect to find not so much cuts or a *dismantling* of the welfare state, but its *restructuring*. The capitalist state, acting in the interests of its national capital, will seek to alter and adapt social policies to suit the perceived needs of that capital. There will, of course, be disagreement between the various representatives of capitalist interests on what these 'needs' are, and different strategies will evolve, some of which are discussed later in this chapter. Furthermore, there will be outright opposition to these pressures from many other groups in society, including parts of the labour movement, something returned to in the next section. But broadly speaking there will be pressure on social policies to aid and abet the accumulation of capital and its reproduction, and pressure to cut back on services designed to 'meet needs' which do not aid the achievement of these objectives. What does this involve?

First, education and social-security policies in particular can be adjusted to adapt the labour force and potential labour force more effectively to the needs of the labour market. Politicians and industrial spokesmen increasingly berate developments in 'progressive' education since the war for producing teenagers unable or unwilling to adapt to the job structure now available. This was put in a particularly blunt way by a research training manager:

> Learning trends in schools are based on participation, liberalisation, humanisation, discovery, de-streaming and the broadening out of the individual. Training and instruction trends in industry appear to be taking the opposite direction towards categorisation, specialisation, control and factionalisation.[18]

We would expect the current crisis to strengthen the hand of the 'industrial trainers' and this is indeed what we find in contemporary Britain. The Labour Prime Minister and the Conservative leadership now vie with each other to launch a 'Great Debate' on educational standards and produce a more 'relevant', 'basic' and 'disciplined' education system.

In social security too we find attempts to harmonise the system more effectively with the requirements of the labour market. Stein[19] divides the devices for encouraging or compelling labour-market activity by public assistance claimants into economic and administrative.

In Britain in recent years we can observe both devices being used. The former include deliberately setting long-term unemployment benefit levels lower than all other benefits (by as much as 19 per cent in 1978) to encourage work incentives, and the introduction of Family Income Supplement in 1970 which has made work a viable alternative to living on supplementary benefits for some segments of the working class, particularly single women with children. Administrative devices such as the 'wage stop' and the 'four week rule', on the contrary, have been relaxed in the face of rising unemployment, but their place has been taken by mushrooming manpower services including job experience schemes and the like.[20]

Not all social services by any means are directed at the working population and the 'reserve army of labour', yet they also perform important roles in adapting or controlling other groups within society. The rapid expansion of social work in the late 1960s and 1970s is partially a response to concern over problem families and their role in perpetuating poverty—and beyond this their lack of control over the behaviour of individual members.[21] The development of community work, community organisations and community development projects in the 1960s was intended to incorporate poorer working-class areas into the restyled local government by fostering a community identification and managing better the conflict between these groups and the various organs of the 'local state'.[22]

A third aspect of the restructuring of the welfare state which we would expect capitalist states to attempt is the improvement of 'efficiency' in the social services. In other words, just as in the capitalist sector, provisions would be made to raise the rate of exploitation of public employees, and we would expect similar measures of rationalisation to be used. This is also what we find. In 1974 the National Health Service was re-organised into larger basic units and a more hierarchical managerial system of control introduced. At the same time, local government was reformed, larger authorities were created and corporate management systems introduced. Within these new large-scale 'service industries', work study and work measurement are increasingly used, especially among the manual and ancillary grades, in order to increase the tempo and intensity of labour and thus to raise productivity.[23] Lastly, the wholesale application of the 'computer revolution' may soon be envisaged within many of the welfare services. All these developments may help redirect expenditure away from labour and towards 'machinery' produced in the capitalist sector. Much of this may well run counter to the interests not only of workers in these services but also of their consumers. In the health service, for example, resentment is increasingly voiced against the impersonal and mechanical treatment of patients inside modern hospitals. If the essence of human services is interaction between provider and consumer, the capitalisation of these services may more and more conflict with the quality of the 'output' provided. The needs of capital for a more cost-effective system comes into conflict with the needs of patients and other consumers.

Lastly, we may expect pressure to develop for the reprivatisation of parts of the welfare state, more specifically for expenditure to switch from direct *state provision* of services to public subsidisation and purchase of *privately-produced* services. The benefits to the capitalist class as a whole of such a policy are by no means clear-cut: in the last chapter the potential benefits to capital of state-produced social services were demonstrated. On the other hand, there are activities, for example house-building, where state production is in direct conflict with capitalist production. In the United Kingdom we may expect to see, for example, growing pressure to curtail local-authority direct works departments. Nevertheless, in other areas the interests of specific sections of capital may conflict with the long-term concerns of the class as a whole, so it is not surprising that opinions are divided. This accounts in part for the long-running debate in the United Kingdom between 'collectivists' and 'anti-collectivists' that has long dominated social policy over the last two decades.

We have noted, then, four ways amongst others in which the state, acting in the long-term interests of capital, may seek to restructure the welfare state at a time of economic crisis like the present: by adapting policies to secure more efficient reproduction of the labour force, by shifting emphasis to the social control of destabilising groups in society, by raising productivity within the social services and possibly by reprivatising parts of the welfare state. All these elements are present in the solution to the fiscal crisis of the state that O'Connor labels 'the social-industrial complex'.[24]

It must be stressed that these are all tendencies which, if our analysis in previous chapters is correct, we would expect to see. All are premised on the theory of the capitalist welfare state elaborated in Chapter 3, as one which continually tends to act on behalf of the capitalist class, to serve the effective reproduction of capitalist social relations and the accumulation of capital. But these are only tendencies and they will be met by opposing counter-tendencies to which we now turn.

CLASS STRUGGLE AND THE WELFARE STATE

There now exists a range of groups seeking to develop the welfare state in quite different directions to those outlined in the previous section. Ultimately the power of all of them is premised on the more favourable balance between the two major classes in advanced capitalist societies since the war, but each has its own specific interests and power. Here we consider the major groups in turn.

First, the growth of public employment, particularly within the social services, has created a new and powerful force with a vested interest in the future development of welfare services. Almost $2\frac{1}{2}$ million people now work in the education and health services alone in the United Kingdom and, very important, a rising share of these have become unionised, By 1975, the major unions in the social services contained the following members:[25]

NALGO	543,000
NUPE	508,000
NUT	264,000
COHSE	143,000

Overall membership has doubled since the early 1960s. The same trend is evident in other countries: in the United States the three fastest growing unions since the war have all been in the public sector. More recently, public-sector unions have displayed increasing militancy and a willingness to use strikes and other forms of direct action previously regarded as unethical. In 1974 some nurses walked out of their jobs and teachers went on strike, hospital doctors have worked to rule and, in 1978, police and university lecturers threatened direct action. Similar developments have occurred in other countries even where the right to strike is legally banned for public employees. In the United States, every federal employee is required to renounce the right to strike, and in 1971 the Supreme Court banned most strikes in the state sector. Yet this has not prevented a veritable explosion of industrial action in the public services there in recent years.[26]

What are the reasons for this growing militancy of social-service workers and what are their strengths and weaknesses? Economic factors are obviously important. Public-sector workers are the first to bear the brunt of any incomes policy, particularly if this is non-statutory, as was the case in the first phase of the Heath government's pay policy in 1971. This led to a pent-up demand for higher wages expressed in the 1974 wage explosion. Similarly, the opportunities for receiving productivity deals to offset pay restraint are much more limited (though not non-existent) in the social services. For the vast number of workers in the manual grades, the rationalisation of job structures and the work process, described above, has generated new forms of shop-floor organisation fighting to oppose these trends.

Among more qualified staff, the same trends towards the routinisation and bureaucratisation of work have clashed with the ethics of professionalism. Doctors, teachers, social workers, nurses and others have developed strong professional associations in the post-war years to serve their interests, among them autonomy and control over their work. But this increasingly conflicts with the demands on the part of the capitalist state for greater managerial control and accountability in the public services. O'Connor expresses this contradiction as follows:

> [Social-service workers] are taught the rudiments of the scientific method, the history of their 'profession', their obligation as public servants, and so on. In the course of their education and work experience service workers learn that their society consists of a system of social relations that can be modified or totally transformed. On the other hand, the fusion of economic base and political super-structure and the fiscal crisis have led to the 'rationalisation' of state jobs, the introduction of efficiency criteria, the waiving of professional standards, and in general the transplantation of capitalist norms from direct production in the private economy to the state administration.[27]

Social workers in the new social-service departments will be acutely aware of these contradictions between expectations and reality.[28] One response to this has been a growing 'economism' in forms of organisation and in demands. Yet the situation will remain ambiguous and a degree of professional autonomy must necessarily attach to all these jobs. Quantitative demands are intermingled with qualitative ones such as the content of education, the structure of medical practice, the goals of social or probation work. Obligations to clients, in however distorted a form, will continue to conflict with the demands of capitalist rationalisation.

These are some of the strengths of organisations representing social-service workers, but there are corresponding weaknesses. The labour force is fragmented by huge differences in qualifications, pay and power between consultants and hospital orderlies, or between head-teachers and school-meals attendants. This is reflected in the host of competing unions and professional associations in each field. Frequently the interests of particular groups conflict with those of other groups and of clients, as with the consultants' support of private practice within NHS hospitals. 'Professionalism' in particular is a double-edged sword here, interfering with unity between employees in a particular service at the same time that it enhances the autonomy of some. Furthermore, the scope for direct action is often limited by the direct harm which it can inflict on clients, patients and consumers. Lastly, any increase in expenditure on a service resulting from such pressure can result in rising taxes which may alienate support from the broader labour movement. These last two points again raise the necessity for a more rounded, political response on the part of social-service workers, which attempts to draw support from both clients and the wider class movement.

Clients' movements and general pressure groups form a second force opposing the cuts and the restructuring of welfare services. The last decade has seen the development of innumerable self-help groups, all of which have called for the extension of some or other aspect of the welfare services: Gingerbread, the Claimants Unions, the squatting movement, Women's Aid and so forth. Sometimes, but not always, these can ally themselves with groups of social-service employees in demanding an improvement in services. Behind this plethora of activity lie more general social movements of which the Women's Liberation Movement is the most important in recent years. All have sought to substitute conscious allocation of resources to meet social needs for the unplanned operation of unregulated market forces.

Behind these social movements, in turn, lies the strength of the organised labour movement. The example of the United States shows how powerful organisations of blacks, women, welfare clients and so on will fail to achieve lasting improvements in social policies in the absence of this bulwark against the power of the dominant classes. Of course, the labour movement can and often has counterimposed its interest to those of such groups, and has even sabotaged the latter. Its policies will depend on a range of national factors, including the degree to which its membership extends beyond the skilled working class. In the United Kingdom in recent years, it has extended its support for a wide range of social reforms and strengthened its opposition to cuts in the welfare state. For example, the 1976 Conference of the Labour Party carried a motion instructing the Labour Government to expand and improve the social services. More significantly it pledged its support

to those Labour Councils which have refused to implement the cuts, and calls on other Labour Groups to follow suit.

A precedent for such action was set by the councillors of Clay Cross, Derbyshire, who refused to implement the Conservative Government's Housing Finance Act and raise council-house rents. At other times specific groups of industrial workers have undertaken industrial action in defence of the social services, as in 1974 when miners in the Yorkshire coalfields struck in support of higher pay for nurses. Numerous examples could be cited from other countries, particularly in Europe, of labour-movement struggles for improvements in welfare services.

Beyond all other differences, those countries with strong trade union and labour movements will tend to oppose cuts and the restructuring of welfare services and to press for improvements and extensions in the welfare field.

But forces are also developing in opposition to more welfare spending and social services. One form that this takes is the 'tax revolt' against the rising burden of taxation. In England this has taken the form of ratepayers associations and has provided one basis for the rise of Enoch Powell and the rightward shift in the Conservative Party. The recent success of Mogens Glistrup in Denmark is another striking example of a populist middle-class party emerging as part of the 'welfare backlash'. The extent of any tax revolt depends, according to a recent study,[29] on the 'openness' of the tax system, in particular the extent to which it relies on property taxes and income taxes, and on the absence of corporatist political structures (something discussed in the next section). In the United Kingdom, where strong trade unions enable many manual workers to win large offsetting wage increases, the tax revolt seems to be based on certain sections of the middle class and especially the self-employed, though its appeal to manual workers should not be underestimated.

This economic basis to the welfare backlash draws on a still thriving free-market ideology, also expressed in recent Conservative Party policies. The objects or victims of its attacks include 'welfare scroungers' and the 'workshy', 'problem families', coloured immigrants, 'soft' social workers, teachers and probation officers, and the 'bloated bureaucracies' of Whitehall and county hall. It propounds an ideology of self-help, independence and reward for effort. Like all ideologies it is based on a partial truth: ultimately the growth of the welfare state in its present form is inimical to both the free-market mechanism and the continued accumulation of capital. Insofar as no coherent answer is offered to the problems discussed in the last chapter, then it will have an appeal beyond the groups traditionally susceptible to such an ideology. This is one of the reasons why, despite the countervailing forces adumbrated above, real opposition to welfare cuts and to unemployment in Britain has been so weak and diffuse. The reality of declining welfare standards and income levels conflicts with an ideology blaming this very decline on the welfare state itself.

CORPORATISM AND THE WELFARE STATE: FROM SOCIAL POLICY TO SOCIAL CONTRACT?

The political and ideological movements referred to immediately above represent a right-wing solution to the current crisis of advanced capitalism. An attack on certain aspects of the welfare state is here coupled with a monetarist economic policy which would rely on 'market forces' (read: higher unemployment) to discipline the working class and enhance profits, coupled with more directly repressive measures directed against the labour movement, such as limiting the right to strike. We have argued that such a policy is risky for the capitalist class and its allies, on both economic and political grounds, particularly in a country like Britain. But there exists potentially an alternative strategy: corporatism and the 'social contract'.

In an enlightening article, Panitch defines corporatism as:

> A political structure within advanced capitalism which integrates organised socio-economic producer groups through a system of representation and co-operative mutual interaction at the leadership level, and of mobilisation and social control at the mass level.[30]

More specifically, it involves

> the integration of central trade unions and business organisations in national economic planning and incomes policy programmes and bodies.

When restricted in this way to the integration within the state of the two basic producer groups in capitalist society—Capital and Labour—it is often referred to as 'tripartism'. The essence of the strategy is that in return for consultation and a 'representational monopoly' within their sphere, each co-party exerts control over the base of their organisaton. In practice, this means that the central union leadership promises to discipline the rank and file membership, notably over pay negotiations and industrial action. It thus provides a mechanism for co-opting the more powerful labour movements in advanced capitalism within the state structure. It is important to stress that this does not mean the state is a neutral body arbiting between capital and labour, though this is of course precisely the impression given by such arrangements. Rather the state, acting on behalf of capital, appreciates the real power of the labour movement and seeks to harness this power in the ultimate interests of the capitalist class.

Corporatism, as defined above, has clearly developed in certain countries with the modern interventionist state since the late 1930s.[31] What is its connection with the rise of welfare states? In Britain, the Second World War saw the Labour Party enter the Coalition Government, and Bevin lead the trade unions into a series of tripartite agreements. It also laid the foundations of the welfare state: in 1942 the Beveridge Report, and in 1944 the White Papers on employment policy and the health service, and the Education Act were all products of this period of corporatist co-operation. Some such as Beveridge saw further ahead to the need for a social contract which would bind the labour movement to a policy of wage restraint in the inflationary years after the war. The *quid pro quo* for such co-operation was full employment and welfare reforms. This formed the basis for the 'post-war settlement' between labour and capital in the late 1940s under the new Labour Government. In Sweden and Norway a similar corporatist strategy developed earlier still, before the Second World War.

In recent years, following a partial reversion to *laissez-faire* policies in the 1950s, corporatism has once more been resurrected as a political strategy within some advanced capitalist countries, and once more it has corresponded with vigorous new growth in the welfare state. The link is this time provided by the growing strength of the working class in advanced capitalist countries as a result of prolonged full or near full employment.[32] This generated persistent inflationary pressures and, at different tempos in individual countries, the state has turned to incomes policies and planning measures to help restrain inflation. According to Warren,

capitalist planning was . . . designed to deal with the economic, as much as the political, consequences of high employment policies after the Second World War.[33]

As we note below this does not automatically generate corporatist political structures—but these

> have been most pronounced precisely in those countries where incomes policy has been at the heart of economic planning.[34]

Sweden, the Netherlands and Britain all provide good examples. Incomes policies directly require the co-operation of trade-union leaders and their willingness to enforce agreements on their members.

In return, improvements in the 'social wage' have often been used as a bargaining counter. In Britain in 1974 this was enshrined in a social contract, which in return for voluntary pay restraint (that did not work in practice) provided food subsidies, a rent freeze and pension increases. A second social contract signed in 1976 resulted in legislation on industrial relations, prices, taxes, nationalisation, employment and training programmes and other areas of social policy, in return for a much more stringent and far less 'voluntary' pay policy. According to a recent survey by Barkin,[35] social contracts have also been implemented in Austria, Belgium, Denmark, Finland, the Netherlands, Norway and Sweden in recent years. All involve a broad agreement between labour unions and the state over a package of measures coupling wage control on the one hand, with social, industrial and economic policies on the other. The 1976 Norwegian agreement, for example, included improvements in family allowances, food subsidies, worker representation in companies, even a bargaining system for creative artists. The Swedish agreements for 1974 and 1975–6 covered a host of social-policy measures including low wages, health insurance, child and housing allowances, pension benefits and the pensionable age (reduced from sixty-seven to sixty-five), security of employment and much more.

It is important to note that such social contracts are not restricted to countries and periods with social democratic governments. Elements of European Christian Democracy and British Conservatism (for example, the Heath–Walker wing of the Conservative Party) also favour corporatist agreements with unions and business organisations. On the other hand, other advanced capitalist countries show no indication yet of pursuing such strategy. In a country such as France, for example, the relative weakness of union structures together with a powerful, centralised state apparatus has given rise to a system of central planning which Shonfield terms 'etatist'.[36] In the United States, on the other hand, one might argue that the late development of a welfare state, together with other special factors, has meant that a corporatist strategy is at present neither possible nor desirable for the capitalist class. These provisos indicate how important it is to separate the development of corporatist structures from the universal centralisation of state structures, referred to in Chapter 4, and the universal development of a recognisable welfare state. The social contract marks a particular response to the development of economic planning and the interventionist welfare state in the post-war period.

If we now return to our arguments in the previous chapter, we can see the relevance of the corporatist strategy to the future development of the welfare state during a period of economic crisis. To put it at its simplest, we argued that a growing level of welfare expenditure need not interfere with the accumulation of capital, so long as the higher 'social wage' could be financed out of total labour costs (the value of labour power) rather than from profits (surplus value). The social contract may provide a means of achieving this and thus of resolving, albeit temporarily, the contradiction within the welfare state analysed earlier. By securing an overall agreement on wages, prices, taxes *and* social benefits, the state may be able to ensure a growing level of welfare expenditure without generating excessive inflationary pressures or harming profitability. The social contract permits the private wage, the 'social wage' and 'collective consumption', plus the level and direction of taxation, to be simultaneously negotiated on a tripartite basis between business, union leaders and the state. This could dampen down some of the conflicts over financing welfare expenditure that have proved harmful to the stability of capitalist economies in recent years. At the same time, by combining this with policies to restructure industry, aid the private sector and channel funds to stimulate investment, this could lay the basis for a renewal of capital accumulation and growth, without encountering some of the risks and adverse consequences of the alternative, right-wing strategy.[37]

If this analysis is correct, the implications for the welfare state are profound. Economically, social policy would become more and more consciously a contingent part of overall economic policy. Politically, the welfare state would both reflect and augment pressures towards the further integration of the labour movement within the state structure of advanced capitalist societies. Social policy would become part and parcel of a social contract between capital, labour and the state. The welfare State would be harbinger to the corporatist state.

But this, too, is to ignore the opposing aspects of a contradictory process through time. When these are taken into account we can also understand the manifest *instability* and *ineffectiveness* of corporatist arrangements in advanced capitalist countries,[38] whether in the field of 'voluntary' incomes policies or in the control of 'grass roots' industrial and political action. First there is the recurring conflict between the 'social wage' and 'social control' aspects of welfare policies. Union leaders will only be able to trade off less money in the pay packet for more social services if the latter are perceived as an unquestionable benefit to their recipients. Leaving aside the possibility of a conflict of interest between working and non-working groups in society, this will itself conflict with the direction in which capital may wish social policy to develop. More means-tested benefits, lower manning levels within the social services and the reprivatisation of some services will not contribute to a higher 'social wage'. Nor *per se* will more social workers (as opposed to home-helps), repressive work experience schemes for school leavers (as opposed to adequate training as a right), or more welfare bureaucrats (as opposed to more comprehensive social-security benefits as of right). Thus a corporatist strategy cannot eradicate the contradictions within the welfare state emphasised throughout this book. If the labour movement secures the better bargain, then the restructuring of the welfare state in the interests of reproduction and capital accumulation will be stalled. If the capitalist class, and the state acting on its behalf, secures the better bargain, then the labour leadership will have great difficulty in 'selling' the terms of the social contract to its membership and in making it stick. At the very least, the price of continued union co-operation in pay and economic policies is likely to be social-policy developments which run counter to those in the long-term interests of capitalism.

Secondly, a corporatist strategy exacerbates the endemic conflict between the leaders and the mass membership of working-class organisations. In the industrial sphere this has been reflected in the growth of shop-floor organisations over the last decade, even in countries like Sweden where centralised wage bargaining has a long history. A social democratic party in power is faced with a continual antagonism between the need to 'deliver the goods' to maintain credibility with its political base and the need to maintain or enhance profitability in order to secure future accumulation and growth. Trade unions facing a social democratic or any other kind of government face a similar dilemma when deciding whether or not to co-operate in some form of social contract. In both cases a gap sooner or later opens up between the social democratic government and the party members, or between trade-union leaders and union members. Specific corporatist structures exacerbate this conflict because their *raison d'être* is a greater degree of control by the leadership over the mass membership. Such a strategy is unlikely to prove stable in the long term.

This is especially the case when a third factor is taken into account: the marked slow-down in growth in all capitalist economies. When productivity increases year by year, even at relatively low British rates, conflicts over social policy and other matters may more easily be resolved. A growing national product permits all groups to gain a larger slice; profits and real wages can both increase over time. This provides the material base for reformism and the welfare state. Now the long post-war boom of the capitalist world has faded and prospects for growth are gloomy. In a period of prolonged recession like the present, the 'need' to restore profitability directly conflicts with the quite different 'need' to improve living standards and levels of social consumption. The material basis for reformism disappears. Social democratic parties and others, including communist parties, who form governments face greater internal strains. So for all these reasons it is unlikely that a corporatist strategy can indefinitely postpone an eruption of class conflict within the advanced capitalist world.

If the long boom of post-war capitalism and the golden age of the welfare state share a common origin, so they may share a common fate. For if the crisis is in any way premised on the power of working-class organisations, then it follows that a long-term solution to the economic crisis must involve weakening their power. It is extremely likely that this will involve an attack not only on recent economic gains but also on the political and social advances of the post-war era. In this process, political democracy and the welfare state will both be vulnerable: their fate will be linked. Capitalism, which in the central countries of Europe and America has permitted the development of the productive forces, political democracy and social rights in the post-war period, may no longer be capable of achieving all three simultaneously. In that case, either accumulation and economic growth or political and social rights must be sacrificed. Either way the nature of the welfare state would be transformed. Contrary to the views of Crosland and others, the welfare state and the mixed economy do not signify the demise of capitalism and the dawn of post-industrial society. The welfare state is a product of the contradictory development of capitalist society and in turn it has generated new contradictions which every day become more apparent.

A POLITICAL POSTSCRIPT

The future development of social policy and welfare state structures in the 1980s will depend on the level and forms of class struggle. In this endemic and ongoing conflict, ideas and theories about the world play a crucial role, and this is especially true in the sphere of social policy. This book has tried to apply Marxist political economy to an analysis of the welfare state. If its arguments have any validity they must be capable of translation into political strategy. Returning to the two radical perspectives on the welfare state criticised in Chapters 1 and 4, we can discern the political implication of each. Those of a socialist persuasion who regard the welfare state as a creature of capital, pure and simple, will have nothing to do with defending or extending it. On the other hand, those who see it as the creation of labour, as a socialist island within a capitalist sea, will fix their standard to the welfare state as it exists. The latter school will be blind to its defects, the former will be unaware of its potential. Neither position, I have argued, is adequate. Once the contradictory nature of the welfare state and its contradictory impact on capitalism is appreciated, then the political strategy of all who work in it, use it or are concerned with it can be refined. The positive aspects of welfare policies need defending and extending, their negative aspects need exposing and attacking. It is at this stage that the concept of 'human needs' becomes relevant in clarifying what is positive and what is negative. In this way, a struggle may be mounted to realise in practice the ideology of the welfare state propounded in many orthodox textbooks: a system for subjecting economic forces to conscious social control and for meeting human needs. It will not develop in this direction without continuous and informed struggle. It is to be hoped that this book will contribute to an understanding of the current welfare state, and hence to this struggle for its transformation away from 'welfare capitalism' and in the direction of 'welfare socialism'.

Appendix A

A NOTE ON RECENT MARXIST DEBATES ON THE CAPITALIST STATE

In the late 1960s a debate on the nature of the capitalist state was initiated between Miliband and Poulantzas.[1] A wide gulf separated their respective positions both on methodology and on substantive analysis. Nevertheless they exhibited an underlying unity, summed up in the notion that the capitalist state was 'relatively autonomous'—both from the economic structures of capitalist societies or 'social formations', and from the politically dominant classes in these social formations. When, in an earlier article, I utilised this common position in order to undertake an analysis of state expenditure in advanced capitalism, this was criticised on various grounds.[2] Several criticisms were based on a 'fundamentalist' approach to certain contentious issues within the Marxist labour theory of value, criticisms which still appear to me to be without foundation. However, the core criticism is correct: that this approach ignores or underplays the link between the nature and functions of the capitalist state and the autonomous dynamic of capital. In emphasising this, the so-called 'German school' of Marxists has rendered a useful service, though I take issue with many of their arguments below.[3] As a result the focus of the debate has switched to that between the structuralist analysis of Poulantzas and the 'capital-logic' analysis of parts of the German school. Or, in Gerstenberger's terms, between the 'class-theoretical' and the 'capital-theoretical' views of the state. In the following, I briefly discuss and criticise each of these, before suggesting the direction in which I believe Marxist analysis should proceed.[4]

The great merit of Poulantzas was in stressing the need for a serious analysis of the political level, or the polity, as something which was not a mere reflection of the economic. Poulantzas defines the role of the state as 'the factor of cohesion within a social formation'. By situating his analysis at the level of social formations, he emphasises class conflict and the role of the state in politically organising the dominant classes and disorganising the subordinate classes. He also takes into account the hierarchy of states at a world level. These are the merits of his approach, but there are several defects. The most important is that for Poulantzas the state is not an institution with power at all: it is a *relation*. The 'state' is generalised to become everything that constitutes the cohesion of a social formation, including the family, religion and so on.[5] Second, this structural determinism also provides a means of avoiding the crucial question: what mechanisms guarantee that the state will operate in the long-term interests of the dominant class? Poulantzas, following Althusser, insists on rejecting the notion of class consciousness here, but the result is, as Miliband points out, precisely the economic reductionism which he wishes to avoid: all the 'effects' of state action necessarily correspond to the interests of the dominant class. Third, the emphasis on class practices sits uneasily beside, or on top of, the underlying structuralist analysis.[6] Class struggle is inserted within Poulantzas' theory to provide a dynamic to the system: the tendential laws of capital accumulation play a subordinate role.

The German school begins by denouncing the very idea of separately analysing the political 'instance' within social formations. It stresses the unique features of the capitalist state as derived from the nature of the capitalist mode of production. The separation of the economy and polity is specific to this mode, not a general feature of all modes. From this stand-point it is able to situate the nature, form, development and functions of the capitalist state within the crisis-ridden development of capital. 'The state can thus be conceived neither as a mere political instrument nor as an institution set up by capital, but rather as a special form of the accomplishment of the social existence of capital along with and besides competition.'[7] On this basis, Holloway and Picciotto[8] and others distinguish three 'moments' of the capitalist state: the establishment of the preconditions for accumulation, the 'liberal' moment when the full separation of politics and economics takes place, and the contemporary moment, dominant from the end of the nineteenth century, when the socialisation of production generates the tendency of the rate of profit to fall. The nature and functions of the state change in each of these three periods.

In situating their analysis of the state within the development of capitalist relations they are thus in a position to consider the changing historical role of the state—a task of great importance. But there are several defects within this theoretical approach. First, despite appearances to the contrary, the logico-historical method espoused here does not satisfactorily deal with the differing origins of the capitalist state, for example in Europe and America. This also means that the state is analysed in the singular, and the existence of a world system of nation states is forgotten. Second, the existence of class struggle is integrated in their analysis in a very functional way, as when Holloway and Picciotto assert: 'In reality, the struggle of the working class, insofar as it is contained within bourgeois forms, merely constitutes part of the political process through which the interests of capital-in-general are established'[9]—so much for the last 150 years of working-class struggle. Third, stress is placed on the limitations of state action as a result of the reproduction of competition capitals within the state apparatus itself. As a result, the ability of the state ever to represent the long-term interests of capital as a whole is denied.

It would appear, indeed, that the class-theoretical and the capital-theoretical approaches share certain errors in common. Neither see the state as an independent subject, capable of facing alternatives, choosing, taking initiatives and even making mistakes. Furthermore, both accord relatively little recognition to the role of working-class struggle in altering the parameters of state action. And, finally, neither show much awareness of the crucial features of representative democracy which functions so well within the capitalist system. The sketch outline developed in Chapter 4 attempts to make good these lacunae and to incorporate the positive features of each approach. As well as these antecedents, it draws on Anderson in recalling 'one of the basic axioms of historical materialism: that secular struggle between classes is ultimately resolved at the *political*—not at the economic or cultural—level of society'.[10] His work also underlies the need for an historical account of the development of modern states which does not ignore the unique origins of each. Lastly, Habermas[11] stresses the way in which 'natural' economic laws are increasingly displaced on to the political plane within late capitalism, recreating the underlying contradictions in new forms. An attempt to incorporate this theoretical development in an analysis of the welfare state is made in Chapter 7.

Appendix B

THE ACTIVITIES OF THE CAPITALIST STATE AND THEIR ECONOMIC SIGNIFICANCE

This appendix links together the classification of state functions and state expenditures in Chapter 3 with the economic analysis of state production in Chapter 6. In both cases a threefold categorisation was put forward and this is set out in Table A.1, together with my application of Marx's analysis of the three 'departments of production'.

Semmler divides all state activities into three functional areas

(*i*) Establishing the conditions of production, such as transport, energy, infrastructure and so forth.

(*ii*) Establishing the conditions for the reproduction of labour power, such as education, health services and so forth.

(*iii*) Establishing the general conditions for reproduction of capitalist relations, such as general administration, justice, police and many other aspects of the general framework within which the reproduction of the capitalist modes takes place. Though he does not say so, aspects of welfare activities may also be included under this heading.[1]

This classification applies to all state activities, including regulatory and administrative arrangements, which do not directly incur state expenditure. They bear a close resemblance, however, to O'Connor's categories of state *expenditure*: social investment, social consumption and social expenses. These have already been outlined in Chapter 3.

On this basis we may allocate the various items of state *production*,

TABLE A.1   *The activities of the capitalist state*

	Contributing to capitalist production	Contributing to the reproduction of the labour force	Contributing to the general reproduction of capitalist social relations
All state activities (Semmler)			
State expenditures (O'Connor)	Social investment—to raise productivity	Social consumption—to lower the reproduction costs of labour power	Social expenses—to maintain social harmony
State production (Gough)	Department I: means of producton Social constant capital— economically reproductive	Department II: wage goods Social variable capital— economically reproductive	Department III: 'luxuries' economically unreproductive
		The welfare state	

SOURCES S. Semmler, 'Private production and the public sector' (unpublished). J. O'Connor, *The Fiscal Crisis of the State* (St James Press, 1973) Introduction and Chapter 4, 5, 6. I. Gough, 'State expenditure in advanced capitalism', *New Left Review* 92 (1975) section v.

that is state-produced goods and services excluding transfers. To do this, I utilise Marx's concepts of 'departments of production', whereby he divides all productive activity into three groups:

(*i*) Department I produces means of production: factories, machinery and so forth. These are the elements of 'constant capital' (*C*).
(*ii*) Department II produces wage goods: all those consumption goods and services, from food to holidays, which constitute the real wages of the workforce of any society at a point in time. These are the elements of 'variable capital' (*V*).
(*iii*) Department III produces what Marx called 'luxuries': goods and services which fit into neither of the above categories.

Within the state sector, the examples of state activities given earlier can now be allocated to each of these departments of production. Of course many will fall into more than one category, as O'Connor points out. Roads and electricity used by industry and commerce are a means of production, whereas that part used by working households are a wage good. The services which comprise the welfare state fall into the second and third categories in all cases, but again there are many problems in deciding where any individual service should be placed, and in most cases they enter both.

This classification is extremely relevant to our analysis in Chapter 6, since the crucial distinction drawn there is between departments I and II on the one hand, and department III on the other. Production in departments I and II is economically *reproductive* or, in O'Connor's terms, performs an accumulation function. Both produce outputs which enter as inputs into further 'rounds' of production and thus provide the material basis for future reproduction (and growth) in the economy: in the first case in the form of means of production, in the second case in the form of a reproduced worker able to perform labour. On the other hand, the output of department III is economically *unreproductive*: these goods and services enter into the production of nothing else at all, even though they may be essential to secure the general conditions for reproduction, such as government administration, the armed forces, various social programmes and so forth. In O'Connor's terms, they perform a legitimation function.

The distinction between reproductive and unreproductive activity is quite different to that between productive and unproductive activity drawn in chapter 6, as the following makes clear:

	Departments I and II (reproductive)	Department III (unreproductive)
Capitalist sector (productive)	1	2
State sector (unproductive)	3	4

All production in a society can be divided into these four groups. The capitalist sector, which in terms of the production of surplus value is productive,[2] produces many goods and services which are unreproductive 'luxuries' according to our definition, such as armaments. Workers in these industries are therefore unreproductive. On the other hand, state workers (excluding those in the nationalised industries) who do not produce an exchange value (a commodity for sale) nor therefore surplus value, may produce crucial elements of constant and variable capital, for example health services. They are therefore reproductive workers.

To understand fully the impact of a growing welfare state within the capitalist mode of production, we need to take both aspects into account. Since state social services do not produce commodities for sale they must be supported out of taxes ultimately levied on the capitalist sector. But since part, though only a part, of these comprise 'wage goods' they play an important role in the reproduction of labour power and hence in the reproduction of capital.

Appendix C

THE STATE SECTOR AND THE CAPITALIST SECTOR

The analysis of state workers in Chapter 6 is elaborated in this note, following the pioneering article by Rowthorn.[1] Surplus labour takes place within the state sector if the labour performed by public employees exceeds the labour time embodied in the goods they consume. This will occur if (*i*) wage levels are comparable (for a given type of labour) with those in the capitalist sector, and (*ii*) productivity is also at the same level as in the equivalent part of the capitalist sector. We shall first assume that these two conditions hold and that all state expenditure is financed via taxes levied on the capitalist sector (whether on capital or labour is immaterial at this stage). In this situation, taxes will be levied to cover the purchases of the state (constant capital C) and to cover the wages of state workers (variable capital V). However, the goods and services produced by them will embody not only the raw materials and labour equivalent of these wages, but also the *surplus* labour performed by these workers. In quantities of embodied labour, the output consists of $C + V + S$, whereas the taxation to finance that need pay for only $C + V$. If we assume that all these services are consumed by workers or capital in the capitalist sector (an unrealistic assumption since, for instance, public employees also use health services), then there is a net flow in embodied labour quantities equal to the surplus labour performed (S) from the state to the capitalist sector. In his original essay on education labour, in which the 'transfer' mechanism is elaborated, Rowthorn expressed this as follows: 'Surplus labour performed in [state] education may be transferred to the capitalist sector where it appears as surplus value, apparently originating there. In reality, however, this surplus value is merely the converted form of surplus labour performed outside of the capitalist sector'.[2] Subsequently[3] he has reformulated this by substituting 'profit' for surplus value. In other words, when we move from the analysis of a pure capitalist mode of production to a complex of different 'sectors' (including the state) within the capitalist mode, profit is no longer simply the 'phenomenal form' of surplus value but the phenomenal form of surplus labour in general. The upshot of this is that the mass of profits *may* be unaffected by the 'socialisation' of any particular industry (some qualifications are discussed below).

Figure A.1 illustrates this point and further develops the analysis by distinguishing the three departments of production.

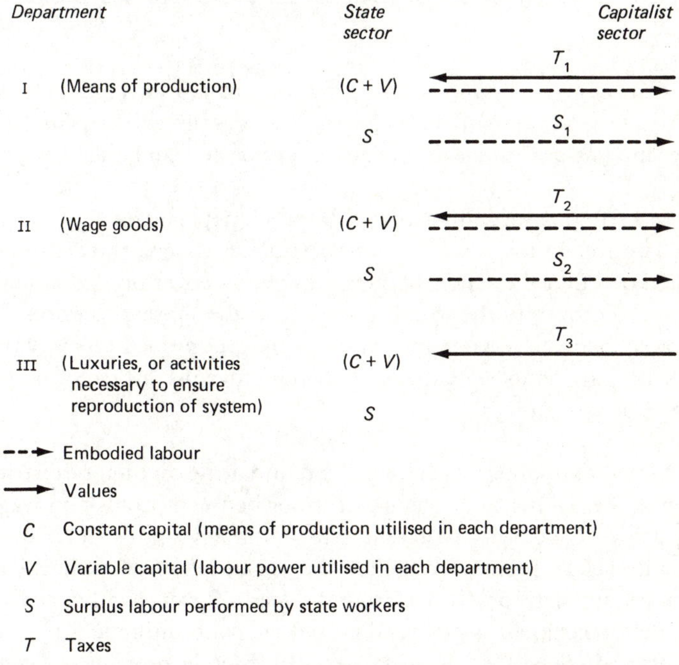

Department		State sector	Capitalist sector
I	(Means of production)	$(C + V)$	T_1
		S	S_1
II	(Wage goods)	$(C + V)$	T_2
		S	S_2
III	(Luxuries, or activities necessary to ensure reproduction of system)	$(C + V)$	T_3
		S	

- - - ► Embodied labour

——► Values

C Constant capital (means of production utilised in each department)

V Variable capital (labour power utilised in each department)

S Surplus labour performed by state workers

T Taxes

FIGURE A.1   *Flows of embodied labour and values*

The argument developed above applies to those state activities which provide goods or services entering as inputs into further rounds of production, that is, means of production or wage goods. In all these cases, 'free' state provision means that the flow of values from the capitalist sector $(= C + V)$ is exceeded by the return flow of inputs, measured in terms of embodied labour *to* the capitalist sector $(= C + V + S)$. However, this does not apply to department

III or unreproductive activities where there is no return flow to the capitalist sector. Here a straightforward drain of surplus value takes place. It will be observed, therefore, that a net flow, in embodied labour terms, *to* the capitalist sector occurs if

$$T_3 < (S_1 + S_2)$$

and *away from* the capitalist sector if

$$T_3 > (S_1 + S_2)$$

The implication of our argument thus far is that the impact of state or socialised production on the capitalist sector depends on two factors:

(*i*) The degree of exploitation (extraction of surplus labour) within the state sector. As in the capitalist sector, this will depend upon the amount and intensity of labour performed and the real wage level (V).

(*ii*) the division of state activities between departments (I + II) and III. The greater the size of the unreproductive sphere, the greater the likelihood that the state will have an adverse effect on the capitalist sector. Turning to the social services, it is the share of services that directly provide services for non-working groups in the population, that is, that cannot potentially contribute to capitalist sector output, which is crucial.

Note that nothing has yet been said about the division or distribution of these flows to the capitalist sector between profits and wages. This is a secondary question but one of immense importance for the accumulation process. Whether the socialisation of a particular service augments or detracts from the mass of profits will depend on (*i*) the department of production and (*ii*) who ultimately pays the associated taxes. Certain social services directly provide use values for the working class and, at the same time, eliminate certain activities from private, profit-making production. But on the argument above, wages may be reduced (or not rise so fast) as a result of socialisation and, if as a result of this the taxes are borne by the working class, the total mass of profits may not be diminished. Indeed, in this case the rate of profit will rise, since the same mass of profits is spread over less capital than before. State transfers, too, must be taken into account when determining the overall effect on profitability and accumulation. The specific areas of the capitalist sector to which state transfers and services are directed will also affect the pattern of the accumulation process. Lastly, all state production will compete with the capitalist sector for labour. If unemployment is low and the wider 'reserve army' is depleted, then this fact alone may outweigh any of the potential benefits of socialisation. But if, for example, the social services draw on a different pool of labour, like unmarried women, this may not be of such importance. All these factors rule out any simple description of state activities as 'unproductive' and detrimental to accumulation and growth.

However, it is necessary to consider here two crucial and related assumptions in the above analysis that have been criticised.[4] The first is the assumption that productivity levels in the state sector are comparable to those in the capitalist sector. Clearly there is a crucial difference between the two sectors in that the 'law of value' or market forces do not operate directly within the state sector. 'The economic activity of the state is not controlled primarily through exchange relationships but through the balance of political (and economic and ideological) class struggles.'[5] In consequence, the unremitting pressure on capitalist firms to lower costs and increase productivity is absent here, so that the 'efficiency' of state production will be considerably lower than that within the capitalist sector. This argument is separate from, and at a different level to, that which emphasises the service nature and labour intensity of many social services. Yet in practice the evidence suggests that many state social services are *more* efficient than their private counterparts: for example the British NHS.[6] Together with the increasing use of techniques such as PPBS, CBA and so forth (see Chapter 7), this suggests that the productivity differential may not be so fundamental a feature as has been suggested.

More damaging is the second and related criticism that the absence of market forces prevents any analysis of flows between the two sectors, for the basic reason that 'values' and 'embodied labour flows' are incommensurable. 'It is only activity under the control of capital that is driven to reduce necessary labour-time to a minimum, creating—through commodity exchange—the category of abstract labour by which particular concrete labours become commensurable as *values*.'[7] If this were true, the opposing flows of S and T in Figure A.1 could not be compared. Undoubtedly, insofar as labour performed within the state is not socially necessary labour time, there is a problem of comparability, but is this the case? The hours, pace and intensity of labour within state services are likely to approximate those in the private sector through the mobility of labour between the two sectors, aided by the adoption of private-sector managerial techniques within the state. And rates of pay within the two sectors have also tended to converge, reflecting the greater mobility of information, if not of managers and workers, between the two sectors. Consequently, it is likely that the ratio of surplus labour, or the rate of exploitation, is converging over time between the two sectors. One can express this more abstractly by observing that the capitalist mode of production is dominant within all capitalist societies, hence it will increasingly determine the labour process and relations of production within the other sectors (or 'forms of labour') in such societies, including the state sector. The growing attempts to 'rationalise' the production process, improve managerial control, introduce efficiency audits and so forth are but expressions of this determining influence. They are also trends pregnant with implications for the future of welfare services.

Appendix D

A NOTE ON THE MARKETED AND NON-MARKETED SECTORS

Bacon and Eltis' analysis of the marketed and non-marketed sectors can be clarified by considering the flows between the expenditure, output and income accounts of the standard national income accounts.[1] A simplified example of a capitalist economy with a large state sector is presented in diagrammatic form in Figure A.2.

It represents an economy that is not growing over time, where aggregate expenditure, output and income all balance. GDP at factor cost = 100 (of whatever unit of measurement). The budget is balanced, there is no foreign trade and there are no indirect taxes. Then, beginning at the left-hand side, total final expenditure consists of C, I and G_r, let us assume in the ratio of 60, 10 and 30. Government resource spending in turn consists of 10 on purchases of goods and services and 20 on wages and salaries of state employees. If we assume that all these state services are not produced for sale, then the output of the non-marketed sector U is 20. The marketed sector produces the inputs to the state sector G_p as well as C and I, totalling 80. This illustrates that it is government employment and the wage and salary levels in the government sector which is crucial in determining the relative size of the marketed and non-marketed sectors.

The next stage considers the division of national output between wages and profits. Let us suppose that the share of profits is an eighth of the marketed sector output. The fact that the non-marketed sector is 20 and that this is entirely composed of wages, means that total wages = 90 and the share of profits in national output as a whole is a tenth. *Ceteris paribus*, the larger the non-marketed sector the lower the share of profits in national income.

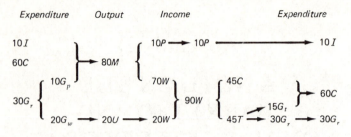

C	Consumption expenditure	M	Output of 'marketed sector' -- that is, commodity-producing sector
I	Investment expenditure		
G_r	Government expenditure on real goods and services	U	Output of 'unproductive sector' — that is, state sector
G_p	Government purchases of commodities	W	Wages
		P	Profits
G_w	Wages and salaries of government employees	T	Direct taxes
		G_t	Transfer to persons

FIGURE A.2   *National income flows*

The third stage looks at how these incomes are spent and returns us back to the expenditure account. Here we must make assumptions about propensities to save and invest, and the burden of taxation. For simplicity I have assumed that all saving is undertaken by firms and none whatsoever by wage-earners, but that all taxation (assumed to be direct) is borne by wage-earners. Firms retain all their profits and invest them again. Wage-earners save nothing but are taxed at a rate of 50 per cent. The result is that $I = 10$, $C = 45$ and $T = 45$. Since the government balances its budget, total state spending $G = 45$, of which $G_r = 30$. The remainder are transfer payments and, to equilibrate our accounts, we assume all these go to households in the form of pensions etc., and none to firms. Thus final consumption $C = 60$, of which 45 is privately-financed consumption and 15 is from transfers, $I = 10$ and $G_r = 30$. Obviously, the state plays an important role at this stage of the process, in determining the burden of taxation, its distribution, the direction of state expenditure (whether towards the household or corporate sector) and its nature (whether resource spending or transfers).

In this hypothetical situation, Bacon and Eltis' ratio of the gross claims of non-producers to marketed output is as follows:

$$\frac{G}{M} = \frac{45}{80} = 56\tfrac{1}{4}\%$$

However, this neglects the fact that state workers also pay taxes, and thus that part of state expenditure immediately flows back again to the Exchequer. Assuming they pay the average rate of tax (50 per cent), then *net* claims of non-producers on marketed output is:

$$\frac{G_p + G_t + 0.5\ G_w}{M} = \frac{35}{80} = 43\tfrac{1}{4}\%$$

(If taxes are also paid on transfer payments, this will further reduce the size of net claims.)

Lastly, we might wish to exclude transfers to persons (G_t) from non-productive claims, on the grounds that they constitute a real benefit to capitalist-sector workers (just as, say, investment grants would be to capitalist-sector firms). If *all* transfers to persons were excluded on this basis, the revised net ratio of non-producers' claims to marketed output would be

$$\frac{G_p + 0.5\ G_w}{M} = \frac{20}{80} = 25\%$$

As Bacon and Eltis point out, the denominator is unaffected by these considerations. It is only the extent of state employment and wage costs which affect the size of the marketed sector output. Thus any increase in state *services*, has a twofold effect:

(i) it increases the claims on marketed output—the numerator, *and*
(ii) it reduces the size of this output—the denominator.

In fact, the share of wages and salaries within total state expenditure in the United Kingdom remained constant over the years that Bacon and Eltis consider. The shares of the three components of state spending moved as follows:[2]

	1961	*1974*
G_w	25%	26%
G_p	37%	30%
G_t	38%	42%

There is no evidence of an 'excessive' growth of state wage payments over this period, the rapid growth of public employment being partially offset by the lower than average increase in public-sector wage and salary levels.[3]

Figure A.2 also helps clarify the three quite different pictures of state activity given in official national income statistics. From the expenditure account we derive the ratio of G_r to GNP, from the output account the ratio of G_w to GNP, and both of these differ from the ratio of $G(=G_r + G_l)$ to GNP which we and others most commonly use (for example, in Table 5.1). As a guide the shares of each in the United Kingdom in 1975 were:[4]

$$G = 58\% \text{ of GNP}$$

$$G_r = 30\% \text{ of GNP}$$

$$G_w = 16\% \text{ of GNP}$$

NOTES AND REFERENCES

CHAPTER I

1. R. Mishra, *Society and Social Welfare: Theoretical Perspectives on Welfare* (Macmillan, 1977) p. 92. I have revised the figure for expenditure on welfare in 1970 based on my own calculations in Chapter 5.
2. R. Titmuss, *Essays on the Welfare State* (Allen and Unwin, 1963) p. 14.
3. F. Lafitte, 'Social policy in a free society', reprinted in W. Birrell *et al.* (eds), *Social Administration: Readings in Applied Social Science* (Penguin, 1973) p. 57.
4. J. Carrier and I. Kendall, 'Social Administration as Social Science', in H. Heisler (ed.), *Foundations of Social Administration* (Macmillan, 1977) p. 27. For a critical dissection of the problems with these approaches to the welfare state see P. Taylor–Gooby, 'The boring crisis of social administration', *Times Higher Education Supplement*, 7 February 1978.
5. It is this which distinguishes the present book from many other radical/critical treatments of the welfare state.
6. The definition propounded by A. Briggs in 'The welfare state in historical perspective', reprinted in C. Schottland (ed.), *The Welfare State* (Harper and Row, 1977).
7. G. Stevenson, 'The social relations of production and consumption in the human service occupations', *Monthly Review*, vol. 28, no. 3, July–August 1976.
8. R. Pinker, *Social Theory and Social Policy* (Heinemann, 1971) p. 144.
9. R. Titmuss, 'The social division of welfare', in *Essays on the Welfare State*.
10. M. Shaw, 'The coming crisis of radical sociology', in R. Blackburn (ed.), *Ideology in Social Science* (Fontana, 1972) p. 38.

11. Ibid.

12. I. Gough, 'Theories of the welfare state: a critique', *International Journal of Health Services*, vol. 8, no. 1, 1978.

13. T. H. Marshall, 'Citizenship and social class', in *Sociology at the Crossroads* (Heinemann, 1963). H. Wilensky and C. Lebeaux, *Industrial Society and Social Welfare* (Glencoe Free Press, 1965). The best short survey and critique of sociological theories of social policy currently available is by R. Mishra, *Society and Social Welfare: Theoretical Perspectives on Welfare*. He distinguishes the citizenship and industrialisation theories from a third school which he regards as properly functionalist. However, this last he himself constructs from the writings of Durkheim, Parsons and others, indicating a 'gap' in welfare theories which he does not explain.

14. See M. Friedman, *Capitalism and Freedom* (University of Chicago Press, 1962) and A. Culyer, *The Economics of Social Policy* (Martin Robertson, 1973).

15. P. Hall *et al.*, *Change, Choice and Conflict in Social Policy* (Heinemann, 1975).

16. See E. Hobsbawn, 'Karl Marx's contribution to historiography', in *Ideology in Social Science*. E. Carr, *What is History?* (Penguin, 1964).

17. This is developed by C. B. Macpherson in 'Politics: post-liberal democracy', in *Ideology in Social Science*.

18. See, *inter alia*, *Income Distribution and Social Change* (Allen and Unwin, 1962) and *The Gift Relationship* (Penguin, 1973).

19. Cf. Mishra, *Society and Social Welfare: Theoretical Perspectives on Welfare*, Chapter 1, who in Chapter 6 also provides a most interesting framework for effecting such a synthesis, drawing on 'Marx, Titmuss and the functionalists'.

20. V. George and P. Wilding in their book, *Ideology and the Welfare State* (Routledge, 1976), provide a most useful foundation for such a study. What they do not do is relate the various ideologies they discuss to the material conditions within (British) capitalism at particular times.

21. It should be evident by now that this book differs radically from orthodox 'economics of social policy', as illustrated for example by A. Culyer's book, *The Economics of Social Policy*.

22. P. Corrigan and P. Leonard, *Social Work Practice Under Capitalism: A Marxist Approach* (Macmillan, 1978).

23. K. Marx, *Capital,* vol. i (Penguin, 1976) Chapter 15.

24. N. Geras, 'Marx and the critique of political economy', in R. Blackburn (ed.), *Ideology in Social Science,* p. 305. The concepts referred to in this passage are elaborated in Chapter 2.

CHAPTER 2

1. Useful introductions to the basic propositions of historical materialism are provided by E. Mandel, *Marxist Economic Theory* (Merlin Press, 1968) chapters 1–5, and J. Harrison, *Marxist Economics for Socialists: A Critique of Reformism* (Pluto Press, 1978).

2. R. Dahrendorf, *Class and Class Conflict in an Industrial Society* (Routledge and Kegan Paul, 1959).

3. K. Marx, *Capital, vol.* iii (Progress Publishers, 1966) pp. 791–2.

4. It will be apparent that the term 'mode of production' is being used in two different senses, to refer to any distinct method of exploitation, and to the *dominant* such method within a society. To avoid confusion I shall use the term in the second sense, and use terms such as 'sectors' when referring to the former.

5. The best introduction to Marxist political economy is still P. Sweezy, *The Theory of Capitalist Development* (Monthly Review Press, 1942). The best modern introduction is M. Howard and P. King, *The Political Economy of Marx* (Longmans, 1975).

6. It is true that this follows from the *definition* of value as socially necessary labour time. The current debate over the labour theory of value and its relation to historical materialism unfortunately cannot be dealt with here. Suffice it to quote M. Dobb, 'Whether human labour is a cost is a practical, not a logical, problem', in *Theories of Value and Distribution since Adam Smith* (Cambridge University Press, 1973) p. 145.

7. This draws on the important article by R. Rowthorn, 'Neo-classicism, neo-Ricardianism and Marxism', *New Left Review,* 86, 1974.

8. E. Mandel in his introduction to the Penguin edition of *Capital,* vol. i (1976) pp. 81–2, lists the first two, but puts as his third condition the compulsion on capitalists to extort the maximum surplus value from the producers. This it seems to me is a consequence of the first two conditions. Moreover, the *ability* continually to do so depends on their ability to introduce new productive techniques which requires their direct control over the production process.

9. See E. O. Wright, 'Class boundaries in advanced capitalist societies', *New Left Review*, 98, 1976.

10. J. Berger and J. Mohr, *A Seventh Man* (Pelican, 1975).

11. I. Gough, 'State expenditure in advanced capitalism', *New Left Review*, 92, 1975, section 3.

12. A. Shonfield, *Modern Capitalism* (Oxford University Press, 1965).

13. E. Hobsbawn, *Industry and Empire* (Pelican, 1969); P. Anderson, 'Origins of the present crisis', reprinted in P. Anderson and R. Blackburn (eds), *Towards Socialism* (Fontana, 1965).

14. J. Stevenson, *Social Conditions in Britain between the Wars* (Penguin, 1977).

15. In *Late Capitalism* (New Left Books, 1975), E. Mandel develops an original theory based on Kondratiev, to explain this periodisation in terms of 'long waves' of upswing and downswing roughly fifty years in duration. This is not the basis of the periodisation put forward here. See R. Rowthorn ('Mandel's "Late Capitalism"', *New Left Review*, 98, 1976, pp. 64–7) who criticises a crucial stage in his argument.

16. E. Hobsbawn, *Industry and Empire*.

17. G. Rimlinger, *Welfare Policy and Industrialisation in Europe, America and Russia* (Wiley, 1971).

18. P. Kaim-Caudle, *Comparative Social Policy and Social Security* (Martin Robertson, 1973).

19. E. Hobsbawn, *Industry and Empire*.

20. S. Marglin, 'What do bosses do?' part I, *Review of Radical Political Economics*, vol. VI, no. 2, summer 1974.

21. K. Marx, *Capital*, vol. I, chapter 10.

22. D. Fraser, *The Evolution of the British Welfare State* (Macmillan, 1973).

23. P. Kaim-Caudle, *Comparative Social Policy and Social Security*.

24. The argument in this section is derived from S. Bowles and H. Gintis, *Schooling in Capitalist America* (Routledge and Kegan Paul, 1976) especially chapters 3, 6, 9. Part of their argument is summarised in S. Bowles, 'Unequal education and the reproduction of the social division of labour' in R. Dale *et al.* (ed.), *Schooling and Capitalism* (Routledge in association with the Open University Press, 1976).

25. H. Braverman, *Labour and Monopoly Capital* (Monthly Review Press, 1974).

26. A. Halsey (ed.), *Trends in British Society since 1900* (Macmillan, 1972).

27. G. Stedman Jones, *Outcast London* (Peregrine Books, 1976).
28. R. Williams, *The Country and the City* (Paladin, 1975) pp. 363, 366.
29. C. Cockburn, *The Local State: Management of Cities and People* (Pluto Press, 1977).
30. D. Fraser, *The Evolution of the British Welfare State.*
31. D. Gordon, 'Capitalism and the Roots of the Urban Crisis', in R. Alcaly and D. Meremelstein (eds), *The Fiscal Crisis of American Cities* (Vintage Books, 1976).
32. The position apparently adopted by C. Offe, 'Advanced Capitalism and the Welfare State', *Politics and Society*, summer 1972.

CHAPTER 3

1. In this section I have drawn heavily on the remarkable introduction by L. Colletti to a recent edition of Marx's early writings on the state. K. Marx, *Early Writings* (Penguin, 1975) in particular pp. 28–46.
2. 'In modern "civil society" the individual appears as liberated from all social ties. He is integrated neither into a citizen community, as in ancient times, nor into a particular corporate community (for example a trade guild) as in medieval times. In "civil society"—which for Hegel as for Adam Smith and Ricardo was a "market society" of producers—individuals are divided from and independent of each other. Under such conditions, just as each person is independent of all others, so does the real nexus of mutual dependence (the bond of *social unity*) become in turn independent of all individuals. This common interest, or "universal" interest, renders itself independent of all the interested parties and assumes a separate existence; and such social unity established in separation from its members is, precisely, the hypostacized modern state' (Colletti, in K. Marx, *Early Writings*, p. 34). The paradox is that the modern state expressing a 'common will' (so beloved by many writers on social policy) only appears with the anarchic unplanned system of capitalism. There is a direct parallel here with Marx's analysis of fetishism, discussed in the previous chapter.
3. P. Anderson, 'The antinomies of Antonio Gramsci', *New Left Review*, 100, 1976–7, p. 28.
4. R. Miliband, *The State in Capitalist Society* (Weidenfeld and Nicolson, 1969).

5. R. Miliband, *Marxism and Politics* (Oxford University Press, 1977) p. 68.
6. Ibid, p. 71.
7. Ibid, p. 72.
8. L. Colletti, in K. Marx, *Early Writings*, p. 37.
9. For an analysis of the role of domestic labour in the reproduction of labour power, see the Conference of Socialist Economists, *On the Political Economy of Women*, CSE pamphlet no. 2 (Stage One, 1976).
10. R. Moroney, *The Family and the State: Considerations for Social Policy* (Longmans, 1976).
11. See here, in particular, E. Wilson, *Women and the Welfare State* (Tavistock, 1977), and 'Women, the state and reproduction since the 1930s', in *On the Political Economy of Women*.
12. Wilson, *Women and the Welfare State*, p. 9.
13. J. Hirsch, 'The state apparatus and social reproduction: elements of a theory of the bourgeois state', in J. Holloway and S. Picciotto (eds), *The State and Capital: A Marxist Debate* (Edward Arnold, 1978).
14. J. O'Connor, *The Fiscal Crisis of the State* (St James Press, 1973).
15. Ibid, p. 6.
16. Ibid, p. 7.
17. See the national case studies in T. Wilson (ed.), *Pensions, Inflation and Growth* (Heinemann, 1974).

CHAPTER 4

1. K. Marx, *Capital*, vol. 1 (Penguin, 1976) chapter 10.
2. Ibid, pp. 381, 382.
3. As do W. Müller and C. Neusüss, 'The illusion of state socialism and the contradiction between wage labour and capital', *Telos*, fall 1976.
4. R. Mishra, *Society and Social Welfare: Theoretical Perspectives on Welfare* (Macmillan, 1977) p. 81.
5. See I. Gough, 'State expenditure in advanced capitalism', *New Left Review*, 92, 1975, section 1.
6. J. Saville, 'The welfare state: an historical approach', *New Reasoner*, 3, winter 1957-8. Parts of this article are reprinted in E. Butterworth and R. Holman (eds), *Social Welfare in Modern Britain* (Fontana, 1975).
7. The best—because historical—comparative study of social policy

to date is by G. Rimlinger, *Welfare Policy and Industrialisation in Europe, America and Russia* (Wiley, 1971). Mishra, *Society and Social Welfare: Theoretical Perspectives on Welfare*, chapter 6, provides an interesting framework for a comparative approach. P. Anderson's two-volume work, in particular his study of absolutist states, *Lineages of the Absolutist State* (New Left Books, 1974), is by far the most impressive Marxist attempt at comparative–historical analysis. His forthcoming volumes on the bourgeois revolutions and on the modern capitalist state are eagerly awaited and should provide a definitive basis for a new comparative–historical study of the welfare state.

8. OECD, *Public Expenditure on Income Maintenance Programmes* (OECD, 1976).

9. Ibid, p. 15.

10. Ibid, p. 12. See also R. Lawson and B. Reed, *Social Security in the European Community* (Political and Economic Planning, 1975), B. Abel–Smith, *Value for Money in Health Services: A Comparative Study* (Heinemann, 1976).

11. For evidence, see Rimlinger, *Welfare Policy and Industrialisation in Europe, America and Russia*; J. Hay, *The Origins of the Liberal Welfare Reforms 1906–1914*, Studies in Economic and Social History (Macmillan, 1975); V. Navarro, *Social Class, Policy Formation and Medicine* (forthcoming); D. Rubinstein and B. Simon, *The Evolution of the Comprehensive School 1926–1972* (Routledge, 1973).

12. R. Miliband, *The State in Capitalist Society* (Weidenfeld and Nicolson, 1969) pp. 16–19; J. O'Connor, *The Fiscal Crisis of the State* (St James Press, 1973).

13. E. O. Wright, 'Class boundaries in advanced capitalist societies', *New Left Review*, 98, 1976—a significant article developing a constructive critique of the analysis in N. Poulantzas, *Classes in Contemporary Capitalism* (New Left Books, 1975).

14. G. Therborn, 'The Rule of Capital and the Rise of Democracy', *New Left Review*, 103, 1977.

15. W. Patterson and I. Campbell, *Social Democracy in Post-War Europe* (Macmillan, 1974) provide a concise survey on which I have drawn.

16. This thesis is argued in 'The crisis of the political party system' by the Bay Area Kapitalistate Group (*Kapitalistate* (forthcoming)).

17. Hay, *The Origins of the Liberal Welfare Reforms 1906–1914*.

18. In the United States, especially, the state is not the sole agency for articulating these interests. The giant foundations and research institutes also perform this function. This undoubtedly reflects the more solid entrenchment of capitalist social relations in the United States and the consequent strength and hegemony of its capitalist class.

19. O'Connor, *The Fiscal Crisis of the State*, in particular chapter 3.

20. H. Glennerster, *Social Service Budgets and Social Policy* (Allen and Unwin, 1975) studies the implications of this for social policy and planning.

21. A. Shonfield, *Modern Capitalism* (Oxford University Press, 1965) chapters 13 and 14.

22. E. Hobsbawn, *Industry and Empire* (Penguin, 1969); P. Anderson, 'Origins of the present crisis', in P. Anderson and R. Blackburn (eds), *Towards Socialism* (Fontana, 1966).

23. Rimlinger, *Welfare Policy*, chapter 4.

24. G. Esping-Anderson, R. Friedland and E. Ohlin Wright, 'Modes of class struggle and the capitalist state', *Kapitalistate*, no. 4/5, 1976, p. 213. See also L. Panitch, 'The development of corporatism in liberal democracies', *Comparative Political Studies*, vol. 10, no. 1, 1977, p. 74.

25. E. Mandel, *Late Capitalism* (New Left Books, 1975) chapter 15.

26. G. Stedman Jones, *Outcast London* (Penguin, 1976).

27. Quoted in Panitch, *Comparative Political Studies*, vol. 10, no. 1, 1977, p. 71.

28. F. Piven and R. Cloward, *Regulating the Poor: the Function of Public Welfare* (Tavistock, 1972) part III.

29. It is derived from a more thorough schematisation put forward by Esping–Anderson, Friedland and Ohlin Wright, *Kapitalistate*, no. 4/5, 1976, in a fruitful article which explores the interconnections between class struggle, state structures and state policies. However, their 'typology of political class struggle' seems to me less sound.

30. Cf. I. Gough, *New Left Review*, 92, 1975, pp. 67–70.

31. Panitch, *Comparative Political Studies*, vol. 10, no. 1, 1977, p. 76.

32. For which see, A. Marwick, *War and Social Change in the Twentieth Century* (Macmillan, 1974).

33. See 'Mandel's "Late Capitalism"' by R. Rowthorn, *New Left Review*, 98, 1976, who provides a concise review of the whole period.

34. This is taken from Shonfield, *Modern Capitalism,* an impressive comparative study of modern capitalism and state economic policies.
35. OECD, *Towards Full Employment and Price Stability* (the McCraken Report) 1977, p. 311.
36. Taken from D. Purdy, 'British Capitalism Since the War, Part 1: Origins of the Crisis', *Marxism Today,* September 1976.
37. Ibid.
38. A Glyn and R. Sutcliffe, *British Capitalism, Workers and the Profits Squeeze* (Penguin, 1972).
39. Emphasised by Shonfield, *Modern Capitalism.*

CHAPTER 5

1. For an introductory account of these concepts see M. Kennedy in A. Prest and D. Coppock (eds), *The UK Economy,* 6th ed. (Weidenfeld and Nicholson, 1976). A more detailed analysis of the relationships between output, income and expenditure in the economy is presented in Appendix D at the end of our book.
2. The difference in the UK figures between the two tables (excluding housing and welfare) is chiefly due to the fact that the denominator in Table 5.1 is GNP at factor cost and in Table 5.2 is GDP at market prices. The former excludes indirect taxes which inflate the values of expenditure items in national income. Note also that the OECD 'average' is the geometric mean, not the arithmetic mean. The same applies to the EEC average.
3. R. Klein *et al., Constraints and Choices* (Centre for Studies in Social Policy, 1976).
4. Comparative data in this chapter is drawn from the following OECD publications: *Expenditure Trends in OECD Countries 1960–1980* (1972), *Public Expenditure on Education* (1976), *Public Expenditure on Income Maintenance Programmes* (1976), *Public Expenditure on Health* (1977), and *The National Accounts of OECD Countries* (various dates).
5. R. Klein *et al., Constraints and Choices,* table 4.
6. R. Klein *et al., Constraints and Choices.*
7. J. Thompson, 'The growth of population to the end of the century', *Social Trends, no. 1* (HMSO, 1970).

8. HMSO, *The Government's Expenditure Plans*, vol. ii, Cmnd. 6721 (1977) p. 80.

9. I am grateful to Ken Judge for help in correcting my original figures for the personal social services.

10. However, compared with net after-tax incomes they almost certainly did rise.

11. C. Trinder, 'Inflation and the social wage', in P. Willmott (ed.), *Sharing Inflation? Poverty Report 1976* (Temple Smith, 1976).

12. For a useful survey, see C. McCreadie, 'The personal social services', in R. Klein (ed.), *Inflation and Priorities* (Centre for Studies in Social Policy, 1975).

13. OECD, *Expenditure Trends*, p. 77.

14. R. Titmuss, *Commitment to Welfare* (Allen and Unwin, 1968).

15. C. Pickvance, 'Physical planning and market forces in urban development', *National Westminster Bank Review*, August 1977.

16. B. Jackson, 'The childminders', *New Society*, 29 November 1973.

17. See R. Moroney, *The Family and the State: Considerations for Social Policy*, (Longman, 1976).

18. This draws partly on work undertaken by the UN and developed in Drewnowski, *On Measuring and Planning the Quality of Life* (Mouton, 1974). P. Knox, *Social Well-being: A Spatial Perspective* (Oxford University Press 1975) and D. Smith, *Human Geography: A Welfare Approach* (Edward Arnold, 1977) provide convenient summaries of the literature on social indicators and levels of living analysis, though Smith's analysis is marred by its eclectic combination with orthodox welfare economics. A Marxist analysis of needs is still awaited, though A. Heller, *The Theory of Need in Marx* (Alison and Busby, 1976) provides an initial foundation on which to build.

19. Ibid. See also, for example, K. Wright, 'Alternative measures of the output of social programmes: the elderly', in A. Culyer (ed.), *Economic Policies and Social Goals* (Martin Robertson, 1974).

20. OECD, Public Expenditure on health, p. 41.

21. This data is drawn from the CSO, *National Income and Expenditure* (various years) and the London and Cambridge Economic Service, *The British Economy*: Key Statistics (various years).

22. OECD, *Towards Full Employment and Price Stability* (June 1977).

23. CDP, *Rates of Decline: An Unacceptable Base of Public Finance* (CDP Information and Intelligence Unit, 1976).

24. Lord Redcliffe–Maud and B. Wood, *English Local Government Reformed* (Oxford University Press, 1974) p. 10.

25. See H. Page, 'Local government in decline' and 'Local government—the final phase?', *Three Banks Review*, no. 90, 1971 and no. 106, 1975. For a detailed Marxist study of some recent developments in local government, see C. Cockburn, *The Local State: Management of Cities and People* (Pluto Press, 1977).

26. H. Glennerster, *Social Service Budgets and Social Policy* (Allen and Unwin, 1975).

27. Ibid, p. 153.

28. J. O'Connor, *The Fiscal Crisis of the State* (St James Press, 1973) chapter 3.

29. H. Glennerster, *Social Service Budgets and Social Policy*, especially chapter 8.

30. This sweeping conclusion clearly needs more systematic comparative analysis to support (or refute) it.

CHAPTER 6

1. G. Maynard and W. van Ryckegham, *A World of Inflation* (Batsford, 1976) chapter 6.

2. R. Sutcliffe, 'Keynesianism and the stabilisation of capitalist economies', in F. Green and P. Nore (eds), *Economics: An Anti-Text* (Macmillan, 1977).

3. The following summarises the argument developed at greater length in an earlier article. I. Gough, 'Marx's theory of productive and unproductive labour', *New Left Review*, 76, 1975.

4. See J. Harrison, 'Productive and unproductive labour in Marx's political economy', *Bulletin of the Conference of Socialist Economists*, autumn 1973.

5. B. Fine and L. Harris, 'State expenditure in advanced capitalism: a critique', *New Left Review*, 98, 1976, p. 106. See also P. Bullock and D. Yaffe, 'Inflation, the crisis and the post-war boom', *Revolutionary Communist*, no. 3/4, November 1975; and P. Howell, 'Once again on productive and improductive labour' in the same issue.

6. R. Bacon and W. Eltis, *Britain's Economic Problem: Too Few Producers* (Macmillan, 1976).

7. Ibid., p. 27.

8. Ibid., pp. 27–8.

9. See C. Trinder, 'Inflation and the social wage', in P. Willmott (ed.), *Sharing Inflation? Poverty Report 1976* (Temple Smith, 1976).

10. It may be thought that this is a separate operation in which the modern state does not intervene, but this would be quite wrong. A major part of savings in Britain today is undertaken through occupational pension schemes, and successive governments have increasingly tied these in with their own social and economic policies. The Conservative and Labour legislation on pensions of 1973 and 1975 now recognises and makes legally compulsory membership of acceptable pension schemes for workers in firms which so choose. Hence employee contributions to these schemes can be regarded as compulsory deductions from their income in no way different to actual taxes. In other words, the 'occupational' and 'social' sectors of welfare, to use Titmuss' terms, have become closely integrated.

11. OECD, *Expenditure Trends in OECD Countries 1960–1980* (1972), p. 56.

12. I have been helped in devising this diagram by Risto Erasaari, who in turn utilised an article by A. Altvater and F. Huisken, 'Produktive und Unproduktive Arbeit als Kampfbegriffe, als Kategorien zur Analyse der Klassenverhaltnisse und der Reproduktions-bedingungen des Kapitals', in *Sozialistische Politik*, Politladen—Reprint no. 19 (Erlangen 1974) p. 367.

13. This distinction, together with much else in this section, draws on recent Marxist analysis of housework and domestic labour. See, for example, S. Himmelweit and S. Mohun, 'Domestic labour and capital', *Cambridge Journal of Economics*, vol. 1, no. 1, March 1977.

14. It is obvious that another very numerous group of workers also produces use values consumed by working-class families: housewives in the domestic sector. For an analysis of the effects of this labour on the value of labour power, see Conference of Socialist Economists, *On the Political Economy of Women*, CSE Pamphlet no. 2, (Stage One, 1976), and Himmelweit and Mohun, *Cambridge Journal of Economics*, vol. 1, no. 1, March 1977. For a different interpretation, see J. Humphries, 'Class struggle and the persistence of the working-class family', *Cambridge Journal of Economics*, vol. 1, no. 3. September 1977. For our purposes we may assume that the proportion of total use values provided by the welfare state is increasing over time by comparison with the capitalist and domestic sectors.

15. R. Rowthorn, 'Skilled labour in the Marxist system', *Bulletin of*

the Conference of Socialist Economists, spring 1974. Some of these issues are elaborated in Appendix C.

16. R. Klein *et al.*, *Constraints and Choices* (Centre for Studies in Social Policy, 1976).
17. See R. Moroney, *The Family and the State: Considerations for Social Policy* (Longmans, 1976).
18. J. O'Connor, *The Fiscal Crisis of the State* (St James Press, 1973).
19. In the process I shall draw on the conflict theory of inflation developed in P. Devine, 'Inflation and Marxist Theory', *Marxism Today*, March 1974, and R. Rowthorn, 'Conflict, inflation and money', *Cambridge Journal of Economics*, vol. 1, no. 3, 1977. See also I. Gough, 'State expenditure in advanced capitalism', *New Left Review*, 92, 1975.
20. This draws on J. Harrison, *Marxist Economics for Socialists* (Pluto Press, 1978) where an analysis of crises of over-accumulation is developed.

CHAPTER 7

1. Much of the data in this section is derived from the Annual White Papers on Public Expenditure, together with the Treasury's monthly *Economic Progress Report*, the *Economist* and various OECD publications.
2. HMSO, *The Government's Expenditure Plans*, 2 volumes, Cmnd. 6721, 1977. The major differences between the 'old basis' and 'new basis' of calculating public expenditure are:

(*i*) Only government lending to nationalised industries is included in the new basis, compared with their total capital expenditure under the old basis. The focus is thus on the demand which the industries make on government funds, and excludes that part of their investment programmes which they finance internally or borrow from non-government sources.
(*ii*) Whereas total debt interest paid by the public sector was included in public expenditure on the old basis, only that part which finances 'social capital', such as roads, schools and hospitals which does not generate income, is included in the new basis. It thus excludes interest paid by nationalised industries, by local housing authorities and other state trading activities which finance their interest charges from sales, rents

or other charges. This change reduced the Government interest item in 1976/7 from £6.5 billion to £1.8 billion.

3. HMSO, Cmnd. 6393, 1976, p. 2. For a Marxist analysis of the restructuring of state expenditure, see the two articles by B. Fine and L. Harris, 'The British economy since March, 1974' and 'The British economy: May 1975–January 1976', *Bulletin of the Conference of Socialist Economists* (CSEB), no. 12, October 1975, and no. 14, October 1976.

4. *Dollars and Sense*, October 1977 (Somerville, Mass.).

5. A. Gamble and P. Walton, *Capitalism and Crisis: Inflation and the State* (Macmillan, 1976) provide a useful survey of these developments.

6. Cmnd. 6721, vol. 1, p. 11.

7. Ibid., p. 1.

8. D. Fraser, *The Evolution of the British Welfare State* (Macmillan, 1973) p. 179.

9. See M. Parkin, 'Where is Britain's inflation going?', *Lloyds Bank Review*, no. 117, July 1975.

10. This and other amusing evidence on the 'ideological offensive' in 1976 and 1977 is presented by K. McDonnell in 'Ideology, crisis and the cuts', *Capital and Class*, no. 4, spring 1978.

11. See H. Glennerster, 'In praise of public expenditure', *New Statesman*, 27 February 1976.

12. The following draws heavily on R. Rowthorn, 'Late capitalism', *New Left Review*, 98, 1976, which in turn is a critical review of E. Mandel, *Late Capitalism* (New Left Books, 1975), and R. Harrison, *Marxist Economics for Socialists* (Pluto Press, 1978), especially chapters 6 and 7. Some of the arguments were developed earlier in I. Gough, 'State expenditure in advanced capitalism', *New Left Review*, 92, 1975.

13. Cf. *Legitimation Crisis* (Heinemann, 1976), where J. Habermas develops a fascinating typology of crises.

14. This draws heavily on an unpublished paper by S. Frith, 'Education, training and the labour process'.

15. Statement by Mr Booth, Secretary of State for Employment, 3 August 1976; reported in *Department of Employment Gazette*, August 1976.

16. HM Treasury, *Economic Progress Report*, July 1977.

17. B. Sutcliffe, 'Keynesianism and the stabilisation of capitalist economies', in F. Green and P. Nore (eds), *Economics: an Anti-Text* (Macmillan, 1977) p. 178.

18. Quoted by S. Frith, 'Education training and the labour process'.
19. B. Stein, *Work and Welfare in Britain and the USA* (Macmillan, 1976).
20. Ibid.
21. E. Wilson, *Women and the Welfare State* (Tavistock, 1977) especially chapter 5.
22. C. Cockburn, *The Local State: Management of Cities and People* (Pluto Press, 1977) chapter 4.
23. See R. Fryer *et al.*, 'Employment and trade unionism in the public services', *Capital and Class*, no. 4, 1978.
24. J. O'Connor, *The Fiscal Crisis of the State* (St James Press, 1973). I have criticised this concept in a review of the book in the *CSEB*, no. 11, June 1975.
25. R. Fryer *et al.*, *Capital and Class*, no. 4, 1978.
26. O'Connor, *The Fiscal Crisis of the State*, chapter 9, provides an excellent analysis of movements within the state sector, on which I have drawn heavily.
27. Ibid., p. 241.
28. A theme of the previous book in this series, P. Corrigan and P. Leonard, *Social Work Practice under Capitalism* (Macmillan, 1978).
29. H. Wilensky, *The 'New Corporatism', Centralisation and the Welfare State* (Sage, 1976).
30. L. Panitch, 'The development of corporatism in liberal democracies', *Comparative Political Studies*, vol. 10, no. 1, April 1977, p. 66. The author acknowledges his debt to an earlier article by P. Schnitter, 'Still the century of corporatism?', *Review of Politics*, 36, January 1974.
31. Corporatism is often associated with the fascist regimes of Italy and Germany, but as defined here it is premised on the existence of independent working-class organisations, and thus on liberal capitalist regimes.
32. I. Gough, *New Left Review*, 92, 1975. In this article I unnecessarily attributed the persistence of full employment to the political commitment of governments to its maintenance.
33. B. Warren, 'Capitalist planning and the state', *New Left Review*, 72, 1972, pp. 3–4.
34. Panitch, *Comparative Political Studies*, vol. 10, no. 1, April 1977, p. 76.
35. S. Barkin in *Monthly Labour Review*, January 1977.
36. A. Shonfield, *Modern Capitalism* (Oxford University Press, 1965).

37. A more detailed investigation of these alternative strategies is provided by R. Bacon and W. Eltis, *Britain's Economic Problem: Too Few Producers* (Macmillan, 1976) chapter 3, and a critique of left reformism by R. Harrison, *Marxist Economics for Socialists*, chapter 7.

38. Panitch, *Comparative Political Studies*, vol. 10, no. 1, April 1977.

APPENDIX A

1. R. Miliband, *The State in Capitalist Society* (Weidenfeld and Nicolson, 1969); N. Poulantzas, *Political Power and Social Classes* (New Left Books, 1973), and the debate between them in *New Left Review*, reprinted in R. Blackburn (ed.), *Ideology and Social Science* (Fontana, 1972).

2. I. Gough, 'State expenditure in advanced capitalism', *New Left Review*, 92, 1975; B. Fine and L. Harris, 'The debate on state expenditure', *New Left Review*, 98, 1976; J. Holloway and S. Picciotto, 'A note on the theory of the state', *Bulletin of the CSE*, no. 14, 1976.

3. See the recent edition of translations by J. Holloway and S. Picciotto, (eds), *The State and Capital: a Marxist Debate* (Edward Arnold, 1978); also E. Altvater, 'Notes on some problems of state interventionism', *Kapitalistate*, no. 1, 1973; W. Müller and C. Neusüss, 'The illusions of state socialism and the contradiction between wage-labour and capital', *Telos*, fall 1975.

4. The most concise survey and critique of Marxist theories of the state is by B. Jessup, 'Recent theories of the capitalist state', *Cambridge Journal of Economics*, vol. 1, no. 4, December 1977.

5. E. Laclau, 'The specificity of the political', *Economy and Society*, 4, 1, 1975.

6. S. Clarke, 'Marxism, sociology and Poulantzas' theory of the state', *Capital and Class*, no. 2, 1977.

7. E. Altvater, *Kapitalistate*, no. 1, 1973, p. 99.

8. J. Holloway and S. Picciotto, 'Capital, crisis and the state', *Capital and Class*, no. 2, 1977.

9. Holloway and Picciotto, 'A note on the theory of the state', *Capital and Class*, no. 2, 1977, p. 5. Also Müller and Neusüss, *Telos*, fall 1975.

10. P. Anderson, *Lineages of the Absolutist State* (New Left Books, 1974) p. 11.

11. J. Habermas, *Legitimation Crisis* (Heinemann, 1976).

APPENDIX B

1. A classification along similar lines is provided in C. Cockburn, *The Local State: Management of Cities and People* (Pluto Press, 1977) p. 53.
2. This is to leave out of account Marx's further distinction between workers engaged in the production and realisation processes. For an analysis that takes this into account see I. Gough and J. Harrison, 'Unproductive labour and housework again', *Bulletin of the CSE*, February 1975.

APPENDIX C

1. R. Rowthorn, 'Skilled labour in the Marxist system', *Bulletin of the Conference of Socialist Economists*, spring 1974.
2. Ibid., p. 31.
3. In a private communication.
4. For example, by B. Fine and L. Harris, 'State expenditure in advanced capitalism: a critique', *New Left Review*, 98, 1976.
5. Ibid., p. 103.
6. See R. Titmuss, *Commitment to Welfare* (Allen and Unwin, 1968) chapter 21.
7. Fine and Harris, *New Left Review*, 98, 1976, p. 105.

APPENDIX D

1. This and Figure 5.2 owes much to J. Hicks, *The Social Framework*, 4th ed. (Oxford University Press, 1971) especially part v.
2. Estimated from the CSO, *National Income and Expenditure*, 1974, chiefly table 9.2. I am grateful to Graham Rodwell for these calculations.
3. See R. Klein *et al.*, *Constraints and Choices* (Centre for Studies in Social Policy, 1976).
4. CSO, *National Income and Expenditure*, 1974, table 9.2.

INDEX

accumulation 156; and alterations in labour force 49; challenges to 65–6; under corporatism 149, 150, 151; and fiscal crisis 127, 132, 136, 152; impact of socialised production on 164–5; as objective of capitalism 12, 13; obligation of state to 43, 44, 50, 51, 123; and state expenditures 14, 102, 105, 108, 117, 122, 138, 145; and state functions 53, 54, 55, 56, 160; and state restructuring 141; and surplus value 25, 26; in world economy 28, 29, 32, 123, 124

action theories: and Marxist political economy 56; of welfare state 8–9

administrative branch: in state structure 41, 42, 63–4

armed forces: depletion of productivity by 122; expenditures on 82; in state structure 41, 42, 63

Bacon, Robert: on de-industrialisation 107–8, 135; on marketed v. non-marketed sectors 106–7, 118, 120, 167–9

boom: bases of 70, 71; contradictions in 123, 124; effects of 72; and fiscal crisis 136

borrowing: financing of welfare state with 94–5; in fiscal crisis 132–3, 134; and state finance 126; and taxation 110

bureaucracy: and social service delivery 94

capital: appropriation of surplus value by 119–20; and class conflict 20, 24, 28, 55, 122, 124, 127; concentration of 27; control of production by 26, 27; corporatist strategy of 146–51; industrial v. banking 73; reproduction of 55, 56, 136–8; reproduction of, v. state activity 158, 159, 161; reproduction of, v. state restructuring 138–41; taxation of 95, 96

capitalism: analysis of, in political economy 5; constraints of, on state 12–14, 42–4; contradictions of 11–12; division of labour under 34–6; dynamics of 25–32; exploitation under 17–20; and fiscal crisis 151–2; and growth of working class 59–60; ideology of 24–5; income flows under 167–8; and Marxist political economy 5–6, 10; mode of production under 20–4; and political rights 7, 39–41, 151–2; proletarianisation under 32–3; short- v. long-term interests of 55–6, 62; and socialised production 162–6; and state autonomy 41–2, 44; and state centralisation 100–1; and state structure 62–4; technological change under 33–4, 35; urbanisation under 36–7; welfare needs generated by 92, 93; welfare state as modification of 1, 2–3; see also monopoly capitalism

capitalism, advanced: accommodation of working class by 69–71; and class conflict 122–4, 127; contradiction of 14; expansion of 123–4; and fiscal crisis 124–5, 127, 131–6; and higher education 35–6; social policy of 9; and the state 155–7; and the welfare state 50, 72–4; and the world economy 71–2

cash: benefits 3, 116; limits 99, 131